Dear Birthmother

Dear Birthmother:
Thank You For Our Baby

by Kathleen Silber and Phylis Speedlin

Second Edition, Revised

Corona Publishing Company
1991

Library of Congress Cataloging in Publication Data

Silber, Kathleen, 1943-
  Dear Birthmother.

  Bibliography: p.
  1. Adoption--United States--Miscellanea.
I. Speedlin, Phylis, 1949-   . II. Title.
HV875.S55 1983   362.7'34'0973   83-1918
ISBN 0-931722-19-5

Cover design by Paul Hudgins

Printed and bound in the United States of America
10 9 8 7 6 5

We dedicate this book to our children
Stacy, Cara, David, Erik, and Sarah.

Acknowledgments

Writing a book and preparing it for publication is a challenging task. We are grateful to the many adoptive parents and birthparents who repeatedly encouraged us to share our ideas back in the early 80's. Without your support, we might always have been "too busy" to meet the challenge.

Our special thanks to Lorraine Babcock, Michele Myers, and Louise Dillow. You spurred us on with kind words and friendship when we might have liked to stop.

To Gail Myers our appreciation and affection. Your expert criticism was invaluable in all that we attempted. Most importantly, thank you for teaching us that we could be advocates of what we believe.

Our gratitude also goes out to David Bowen, our publisher and friend. You helped transform our ideas and words into the reality of a finished book.

Since *Dear Birthmother's* initial publication in 1982, we have heard from hundreds of birthparents, adoptive parents, adoptees, and adoption professionals, sharing personal stories and thanking us for being "brave enough" to challenge traditional adoption practice and for pioneering a more humane and open form of adoption. We appreciated your feedback over the past decade, each letter or call reminding us of the pain of closed adoption and the power of open adoption. Many of you have told us that *Dear Birthmother* changed your lives (for the better), and that was our hope when we wrote this book. Your letters, and the dramatic movement we have seen in adoption practice around the country, have been wonderfully gratifying.

This revised version of *Dear Birthother* reflects the changes which have brought open adoption practice into the 1990's. Our special thanks to Patricia Dorner for your help and advice as we prepared this new edition. We also sincerely thank the adoptive parents and birthparents who updated their stories and those who shared new stories.

We especially thank our husbands, Herbert and Richard. Your understanding, patience, and love sustained us during the years we worked on this book.

This is truly the decade of open adoption.

Kathleen and Phylis
January 1991

CONTENTS

Introduction

Dear Reader,

 Dear Birthmother, which was initially published in 1982, explores some of the myths in adoption and details the evolution of open adoption, from letter exchanges to face-to-face meetings and ongoing contact. *Dear Birthmother* has had a tremendous effect on adoption practice nationwide, resulting in a significant shift from traditional adoption to open adoption. In 1982 only a handful of agencies practiced open adoption, compared to today when most adoption agencies and intermediaries offer at least some components of open adoption. However, since the initial publication of *Dear Birthmother*, open adoption has also continued to evolve. This book will examine the theoretical basis for open adoption and its evolution. We also refer our reader to a sequel, *Children of Open Adoption*, by Kathleen Silber and Patricia Martinez Dorner (published in 1990), which follows some of the participants in *Dear Birthmother* and which also explores the lifelong impact of open adoption on all parties, particularly the adopted children.

 The ideas we hope to share with you in *Dear Birthmother* began to take shape many years ago when one petite and determined young birthmother helped our adoption program take some dramatic steps forward. After writing a letter to the adoptive parents of her child, a practice we had been allowing (but not encouraging) for several years, this birthmother asked the unthinkable question, "Will you ask them to write me back? I want to know what they think about my baby. I want to know if they could possibly love him as much as I do."

In the 1970's, there was almost no such thing as an "open" adoption. Official records were, and still are in most states, sealed by the courts; communication of any sort between birthparents, their offspring, and their adoptive families was discouraged by laymen and professionals alike as "dangerous." But what is an open adoption? What is this thing which was labeled dangerous and unnatural when *Dear Birthmother* was first published in 1982 and which still remains a shocking concept to many people? The answer is so simple it is disarming. "Open" merely refers to open channels of communication between birthparents and adoptive parents. In addition, in open adoption, all of the choices and control are in the hands of the adopting parents and birthparents themselves, rather than the adoption intermediary.

The wisdom of the past dictated that, in matters of adoption, secrecy was of paramount importance; barring emergency medical considerations, there should never be contact between any of the parties involved after the legal relinquishment. For many years there were valid sociological reasons for this rigid standard; in recent years, however, it has become apparent that the traditional "closed" system of adoption is fraught with dangers of its own. In our experience with open adoption, we have found that the exchange of information between birthparents, adoptive parents, and adoptees has eased a great deal of the trauma associated with the closed system. The times have changed, and today people are more satisfied with a process that is founded upon simple openness and honesty rather than an artificially built up emotional mythology.

I am Kathleen Silber. I am the Associate Executive Director of the National Federation for Open Adoption Education and the Independent Adoption Center in Pleasant Hill, California, but my work in open adoption began in Texas in the 1970's (and my work in traditional adoption began in the 1960's). When we facilitated that first letter exchange, its impact on the people involved was obvious and immediate. I began to question traditional agency practices and my own professional attitudes toward adoption. I knew, of course, that birthmothers were not the "uncaring baby machines" society generally supposed them to be, and yet I had followed the traditional adoption philosophy which demanded that the birthmother be cut off from her child as completely as possible. I had seen the fear felt by adoptive parents that the birthmother would someday return to snatch up "her" child, and I said "She doesn't want to remember this part of her life; she will forget."

What struck me in watching the first exchanges of letters was how healthy it all seemed—how relieved everyone was. The adoptive parents were relieved to find that among the genes carried by their adopted child, there were none from an uncaring baby machine, and quite happy to hear the birthmother's assurances that she would never invade their lives. The birthmother, in turn, was overjoyed to hear that her child was well loved, happy, and healthy. Now that open adoption has been practiced for many years, we also know that the adopted child is much happier and emotionally more stable knowing that his birthparents had indeed loved him very much (and still love him).

I left Texas in 1986, and I am now associated with another pioneering open adoption program in California—a nonprofit independent adoption organization which offers open adoption with professional counseling, education, and support. There are some distinct differences between agency and independent adoption, as well as differences in the type and quality of adoption services available from one community to the next. However, I encourage all adoption intermediaries—whether they are agencies or independent practitioners—to offer open adoption with comprehensive counseling services and with the control being in the hands of the adoptive parents and birthparents (*not* the intermediary). I also encourage adoptive parents and birthparents to become educated consumers and to seek out adoption programs which offer these essential ingredients.

Since *Dear Birthmother* was originally published I have also evolved in my thinking about open adoption. I am more committed than ever to this practice, which is truly more responsive to people's needs, as well as more honest and humane. I have personally been involved with several hundred open adoptions, and I have observed that they include a lot of love and caring, rather than fear and mystery which have traditionally surrounded adoption. As a result of my experiences, I advocate meeting in person, sharing full identifying information, and engaging in ongoing contact over the years (either through correspondence or in person). I think it is preferable for all parties to have direct access to ongoing contact and to be in control of their lives, rather than at the mercy of laws, agency regulations, or agency personnel (all of which can change over time). I further believe that open adoption is the hope of the future for the field of adoption.

I am Phylis Speedlin. My husband and I adopted our first daughter, Stacy, 13 years ago. Before Stacy's adoption, our opinion of birthparents was ill-defined. Our fantasies about these people ranged from the birthmother being a fertile but uncaring woman to the birthfather being an irresponsible cad. Our most frightening vision was that they both were indecisive about their decision to place Stacy. Could they become villainous kidnappers who would one day reappear to claim their own?

Our thoughts and fears about Stacy's birthparents were not lessened by the circumstances of her adoption. Stacy's placement with us was closed. We lived with ill-founded ideas about her birthmother, as her birthmother undoubtedly lived with incorrect assumptions about herself. By the time we had come to realize from talking to many adoptees that Stacy would need contact with her birthmother—and, in fact, the birthmother needed contact with Stacy, no matter how remote—the closed system had done its best to complete the closure. When contacted three years after the placement, the pain and guilt that Stacy's birthmother felt over the matter were such that she did not even want to open the letter we sent.

Open adoption became necessary for Stacy soon after her 8th birthday. On the morning of her special day, my husband and I found her in tears before her bathroom mirror. "My birthmother gave me away because she is blond and I am not." The depth of her despair tore our hearts. How could such a beautiful dark-haired girl believe she was rejected because of her looks? Why had none of the information we so freely gave soothed her hurts?

At that time, we sought an intermediary to locate Stacy's birthparents. The adoption agency resisted, but we were protecting our daughter, so we persisted. (I admit our persistence was not without fears because these agency people were the "experts.") Once contacted in person, Stacy's birthmother was at first open and then closed to face-to-face contact with us and/or Stacy.

Our question then became do we persist and approach Stacy's birthfather? Again, the agency said "no" and warned us that this would cause serious problems. Stacy, however, was still in pain, and we wanted answers for her. Finally, our intermediary contacted Stacy's birthfather, and it was better than we could have imagined.

Here was a man who had made the decision not ever to move or change his phone number in hopes "one day" his daughter would seek and find him. Through our intermediary, we met Stacy's birthfather—first without Stacy being present. Our meeting confirmed that he loved his daughter and would be good for her.

We also placed Stacy with a child therapist to determine if she could handle an "opening" adoption at the age of 8-1/2 years. After several meetings with the therapist, the day was set—Stacy would meet her birthfather "face-to-face."

How nervous we all were! How Stacy talked and talked, and how her birthfather loved her with his eyes. After that first meeting, Stacy's birthfather seemed to be a natural part of our lives. That first Mother's Day, he sent me a beautiful flower arrangement and said, "Thank you for being Stacy's mom."

Subsequently, on birthdays and at Christmastime, he would come to our home for a short visit. At first, the visits were always with us present. This was to confirm for Stacy that we were and always would be present. She did not have to choose between her adoptive parents and her birthparents.

For Stacy's 12th birthday, however, she asked to go to Sea World in San Antonio with her birthfather and her biological sister. The three of them had a wonderful day. Regrettably, Stacy's birthmother was never comfortable with open adoption, although she has met Stacy and spoken with her on the phone. I strongly believe that had she been adequately counseled at the time of Stacy's birth, had she known that she did not have to "forget" her child (as society demanded of her), then openness would not pose such a problem for her.

Stacy's sister, Cara, was adopted 11 years ago. By contrast to Stacy, Cara had from her placement a picture of her birthmother, a gift from her birthmother, and a letter telling her how much she was loved and how sorry her birthparents were that circumstances would not allow them to parent her. Within a few years of her placement, Cara's adoption opened further. Phone contact and then a face-to-face "adventure" at Disneyland provided Cara answers to many of her remaining questions. There is no doubt in anyone's mind where Cara gets her physical characteristics and impish personality!

As an adoptive parent, I know that adoption is much more than simply the placement of a long-awaited child. It is a lifetime experience for the adoptive parents, the adoptee, and the birthparents. I am absolutely convinced that for all parties involved, that experience must be open.

This letter from us serves as an introduction to the many beautiful letters included in *Dear Birthmother*. These are the original letters; we have not altered their spelling, grammar, or content in any way. Some letter writers requested that we use their real names, others that we change them; their preferences have been followed.

Our intent when we began to write this book was to share with our readers a sampling of the letters we had seen exchanged through our adoption program. Our goal was to show the warmth, trust, and love possible between birthparents and adoptive parents when given the opportunity to communicate in the form of a letter. In the beginning, these letters were exchanged without any identifying names or addresses, with the agency acting as intermediary. Later, individuals chose to be in direct contact with one another. Initially, however, many people who read or heard about this form of communication reacted strongly against the idea of even minimal contact between birthparents and adoptive parents. Their reactions could be divided into four typical concerns or assumptions about the adoptive relationship. What surprised us most, though, was that these same four concerns and assumptions seemed to account for much of what we considered our professional attitudes toward adoption and standard agency practices.

As a result of this insight, we redesigned *Dear Birthmother* from a simple collection of letters to include a presentation of the four "myths"(as we now call them) which we had uncovered. It seemed clear that many of the most common emotional problems associated with the closed system of adoption actually stemmed from these myths. Therefore, we wanted to offer solutions, or at least alternatives, to the status quo. The second half of our book evolved during our attempt to arrive at specific recommendations for a myth-free adoption program.

While there have been no long-term psychological studies, we are committed advocates of a new approach to adoption because of the very real benefits it offers in human terms to those personally involved. This new approach includes, as a basic ingredient, open adoption. In 1982, we defined open adoption as any form of communication between birthparents and adoptive parents, either directly or through an intermediary. However, as the practice of open adoption has continued to evolve over the years, so has its definition. Today we distinguish between openness in adoption and open adoption:

> Openness in adoption (or semi-open adoption) refers to various forms of communication between birthparents and adoptive parents, such as exchanging letters and pictures, meeting on a first-name-only

basis, meeting once but not engaging in ongoing contact, etc. In these situations, the primary control remains in the hands of the adoption intermediary.

Open adoption includes the birthparents and adoptive parents meeting one another, sharing full identifying information, and having access to ongoing contact over the years (all three components must occur to fit this definition).* The form of ongoing contact (letters or visitation) and the frequency are determined by the individuals involved in each particular case. In open adoption all of the control and choices are in the hands of the adopting parents and birthparents, rather than the adoption intermediary.

Since this book describes the beginnings and evolution of open adoption, most of the adoptions discussed are semi-open ones. Open adoptions are discussed in the latter part of the book, as well as in *Children of Open Adoption*.

Our experiences have been primarily with infant adoptions and voluntary placements. Although we have not addressed adoptions of older children or involuntary placements, we do feel that open adoption in these situations is also beneficial.

Not every birthparent or adoptive parent will be comfortable with the open practices our work presents. Millions of adoptions have taken place in this country under the closed system, all with the laudable goal of providing homes for children whose birthparents, for one reason or another, could not parent them themselves. It is our fervent wish that *Dear Birthmother* not become a source of guilt or confusion to the birthparents and adoptive parents who have experienced traditional closed adoption. Like most human interactions, adoption is an evolving and dynamic process. As attitudes change and society redefines its value system, what came before is simply history—not something to be denigrated or scoffed at. Given the way our society feels about children

---

*Silber, Kathleen and Patricia Martinez Dorner, *Children of Open Adoption*, San Antonio. Corona Publishing Co., 1990.

today, what would we say to the Victorian lady who gave her children up almost immediately to a wet-nurse, then had them raised by a nanny, then sent them off to a boarding school? She was not evil for doing so—in fact, she was probably trying to be the best mother she could be by following what society deemed best for the child. Society now demands openness and honesty in human relationships; we feel that adoption practices should reflect this.

We also advocate open adoption accompanied by comprehensive counseling, educational, and support services. We encourage our reader to seek out an adoption intermediary which offers these essential ingredients to a successful adoption.

The letters published in *Dear Birthmother*, as well as our letter here to you, are based upon the simple concept of open communication and trust. These letters reinforce our commitment to an enlightened adoption process. We invite you to sample these letters and to savor their humanity.

Sincerely,
Kathleen and Phylis

Part One:
Four Myths
Of
Adoption

Until recent years, most adoption agencies and intermediaries followed traditional adoption practices. For birthparents, this meant that the focus of adoption counseling was on the pregnancy and eventual relinquishment of parental rights. Direct interaction with birthmothers and birthfathers revolved primarily around this decision-making process. We did not discuss or prepare these individuals for any aftermath to their decision because we expected our birthparents to go home after terminating their parental rights, forget their untimely pregnancy, and proceed with their own lives.

Our work with adoptive parents also progressed in accordance with professionally approved methods. Applications from prospective adoptive parents were periodically accepted based on the projected availability of infants. If the couple met agency eligibility requirements and passed some initial screening, they were given a formal application for adoption through the agency. Once they completed all necessary paperwork, the couple was assigned a social worker. The social worker would then conduct office interviews and arrange home visits in order to determine the couple's emotional, marital, and financial stability. Their suitability as parents was also evaluated. However, issues the couple would surely face as adoptive parents were not discussed, and birthparents were rarely mentioned. Assuming the couple passed our criteria, they were "approved" and placed on a waiting list—sometimes waiting several years. Eventually a child was placed with them, but this did not signal the end of our involvement. During the statutory waiting period before the adoption could be legally finalized in court, the social worker again visited the couple's home, this time to determine how they were doing as parents. With the final court appearance, our involvement did end. Court records were sealed, our extensive agency files were closed, and we assumed the new family would "live happily ever after."

What we failed to realize was that the standards for our birthparent and adoptive parent programs stemmed from a series of stereotypical misconceptions that have historically surrounded adoption. Today, we are acutely aware of how four such stereotypes persist and dominate adoption practices. We refer to these stereotypes as the four myths of adoption. They represent impressions and assumptions formed partly from media influences, and partly from half-remembered, indifferently accurate, and ambiguously reported stories. Regrettably, these fictions are persuasive, easily understood, and easily passed along. You, as our reader, may cringe as you read indictments against your own attitudes about the people who play out the adoption story.

The four myths of adoption are:

1. **"The birthmother obviously doesn't care about her child or she wouldn't have given him away."**

2. **"Secrecy in every phase of the adoption process is necessary to protect all parties."**

3. **"Both the birthmother and birthfather will forget about their unwanted child."**

4. **"If the adoptee really loved his adoptive family, he would not have to search for his birthparents."**

In the next four chapters we will explore with you the awesome influence that each myth has on adoption. We offer you our experiences and evolution, and the poignant thoughts and reactions of people who are living today's adoption drama. You will have the opportunity to see deeply into the lives of birthparents and adoptive parents. Mothers who "give away" a child to another set of parents to nurture can make you weep with the depth of their love—for the child and for the new parents. Adoptive parents who share their infertility experience and grief will deeply touch you even if you think you have no interest in adoption.

Our clients are not all highly educated or insightful. They come from various socio-economic levels. These individuals, in fact, typify the women and men involved with adoption daily throughout the United States—with one exception. Each of our clients has been encouraged to deal with their untimely pregnancy or their infertility in a myth-free manner.

1
Dear Birthmother,
We Know You Care

Myth Number One:
*"The birthmother obviously doesn't
care about her child or she wouldn't
have given him away."*

People accept the first myth of adoption as true because they make the following assumptions about the birthmother:

- She is able to ignore the first stirrings and movements of life within her body.
- She is able to forget the beauty of creation and the actual birth experience.
- She is able to disregard the sight of a beautiful newborn baby.
- She is able to suppress the innate yearnings to nurture her child.
- She is able to dismiss the fantasies, hopes, and dreams she may have had for her child's future with her.
- She is able to ignore the pain of signing a relinquishment document, knowing that all her legal rights to her child are forever terminated, and that she has sealed her child's future for better or for worse.

Until you meet someone like Lindy, you can more readily accept such assumptions and believe that birthmothers do not care about the life they can "so easily" give away. Lindy was a young woman four months pregnant when we first met her. The months of pregnancy had emotionally drained Lindy because she loved the little life growing and moving within her body. Throughout her pregnancy, Lindy struggled with her own feelings and the conflicting pressures of family members. The day her son, Noah, was born, Lindy felt true joy at seeing him alive and healthy, and hearing his first cry. She protectively cared for Noah during her three-day hospital stay, and then arranged a unique religious service to be held in the hospital chapel. The service was held on the day she last saw Noah, to bless him and his future with his "new parents." That service was Lindy's special goodbye.

Certainly, Lindy's actions cannot be described as irresponsible or uncaring. She, in fact, struggled for nine months to come to terms with Noah's existence separate from hers. It took all her courage to sign the relinquishment papers that placed her son for adoption.

The depth of Lindy's love for Noah and the conscientiousness of her decision is best reflected in this letter, written to her son shortly after birth:

> To a very special boy,
>
> I don't quite know how to begin this letter, except to say that I love you very, very much.
>
> I will try to write this letter so that you will understand fully the reasons I chose adoption for you.
>
> I was 19 at the time you were conceived. I was very young and disillusioned about love. I was going through a hard period in my life. I was not communicating with my parents. So I reached out to whatever love I could find.
>
> I met your father in the summer . . . We dated for about two months and we broke up. After 1-1/2 years, in December we started dating again.
>
> I was really having problems with my parents so I moved in with your father. I was very much in love with your father. Your father and I were different in many ways. We had different ideas about love, and after 5-1/2 months I moved home to my parents. Shortly after, I discovered I was pregnant.

I can hardly describe my feelings. I was filled with joy and sorrow.

I was so happy to be carrying you, and I was sad because your father was involved with someone else. I told your father about you and we talked and decided that marriage would not be fair to anyone, especially you.

After I told my parents (your birthgrandparents) they were deeply hurt. They are very old fashioned and religious. After much discussion we all agreed that I should go to live with my sister 1200 miles away.

As I approached the mid-term of my pregnancy, I was faced with the fact of how to raise you. I wanted so badly to keep you and protect you, but the fact that I had no money, no job, and no place to live, I decided for adoption. No matter how dearly I love you, I was going to have to choose adoption so that you could live a full and happy life. That's all I wanted, was for you to be happy and to have so many things I couldn't provide. I couldn't live with myself, if I weren't able to give you everything you need and want. So you see, adoption was the right choice. You have a loving family and two beautiful parents who love and adore you as much as I do.

If you were able to live on love, there would be no problem. Because I have so much love in my heart for you, you'll never know. But you're not able to live on love alone, and as much as it hurts me to admit it, that is all I could have gave you. It's just not enough. But I wish it was. There was no reason for you to suffer because of my selfishness. Try to understand I did it because I love you so very much.

As time went by I got very fat! And on March 26, at 6:25 P.M. I delivered the most beautiful 6 lb. 7 oz. baby boy. I was so proud and I was filled with joy. You were so tiny and beautiful. I couldn't believe I had given birth to such a beautiful and perfect little boy. I thank God every day for you. I am still proud of you and think of you every single day. I wonder what you're doing and what you look like.

I stayed at the hospital for three days. During my stay I fed you, held you, and prayed for you. I'll never forget the first time I held you. You threw up all over me. HA-HA! But it was O.K. You could really make some funny faces. I took dozens of pictures. You were so cute! The day finally came (too quick) for me to go home. On March 29th I signed relinquishment papers, giving you the right to a full and happy life. It was the hardest thing I've ever done.

We held a special service for you in the chapel of the hospital. A friend bought a gown for you, and a bonnet and we dressed you up and we all prayed that you would have the life you deserved. You were so beautiful in that gown. So fragile and pure. I love you.

As I saw you for the last time I realized I should not be sad, but be thankful that you have two beautiful parents that love and adore you very much. I know that you will bring them an unmeasurable amount of joy and happiness.

I hope this letter will clear up any doubts of my love for you, or any questions you might have. I would like you to know that if you ever decide to try and find me, please do!! I'll be waiting anxiously if you ever decide to. It would be a dream come true. But the decision's yours and I'm sure your parents will be open and supportive of any decision you make. If you choose not to see me, I'll try to understand.

I hope I've said the right thing to make you realize I really do love you! You've brought me so much happiness that I can't even describe. I hope someday that I'll be able to bring you happiness by being your friend. Please understand that I don't want to interfere in your life, or come between you and your parents. I don't want to be a threat to your relationship with your parents.

I know this letter is probably going to be a shock. I don't want to hurt you. I just want to love you, and I do with all my heart. If and when you decide to see me, please talk openly with your parents. Get their opinion.

But whatever happens, know that I will always be here, forever.

As I come to a close, I realize that this may be the last time I'll ever be able to express my feelings to you, so once again I'll say I'll be here forever and ever. I love you so very, very much. Never forget that.

God bless you and your adoptive parents. I love you all very much.

> Love,
> Your Birthmother
> Lindy

As her letter illustrates, Lindy was not able to ignore the fact that she had created life or to forget the experience of nurturing her "beautiful and perfect little boy." Contrary to the first myth, she responded to her pregnancy and to Noah with deep maternal feelings. Lindy's decision to place Noah for adoption does not somehow magically erase those feelings.

Lindy wrote a second letter to Noah's new parents four months after Noah's birth. This second letter by Lindy shows just how unselfish and painful the decision of adoption can be for a birthmother:

Dear Patti and John,

Over the past few months I've been trying to figure out what to write. First of all I'd like to thank you for giving Noah a loving home. I'm sure he will bring great happiness and joy to you in the years to come.

You both know a little about my family. I'm the baby of six. There are 5 girls and 1 boy. As you already know, my real father died when I was very young. I don't remember him at all. I was brought up by a wonderful step-father, who I consider as my real father. My father was very protective of me. And as I grew older it was hard for him to accept the fact that his little girl was growing up. Like most teenagers I went through a period of rebellion. I fought with my parents, and I lost all communication I had with them.

After my 19th birthday, I moved out of my parents' house and moved in with my baby's father. We both had different ideas about love and to say the least, our love didn't last very long.

After 5 months, I moved back to my parents house I soon discovered I was pregnant. It hit me hard. I had mixed emotions about my pregnancy.

After much thought and discussion, I decided for adoption. There's so much I want Noah to have that I can't provide like a stable home life. I want you to know I feel very secure about my decision.

I'll tell you a little bit about my pregnancy. First of all I got very fat! HA-HA! I had morning sickness a lot. I also was very content in bringing this child to you. At times I feel sad, but then I think about the love he's giving and receiving. Deep in my heart I know he's getting all the love that two people can give. I have peace inside knowing Noah is with a real family.

There is one thing I feel I must tell you. I was never very close to my parents, so I ask you to always be open and honest with him. Never lose communication with him. I never realized how important that was until I lost what little communication I had. I know now, because I learned the hard way.

I hope you'll respond to this letter and if it's not too much to ask, could you please send me a picture. I would really appreciate it.

I'd like to thank you for the chance to express my feelings. I am really grateful and I want you to know that even though we've never met, you both

have very special places in my heart. You always
will.

Thank you again for giving Noah all your love.

Please write back and send a picture.

I Love You! Here's a picture of the last time
I saw him!

Lindy

P.S. Did you get his bonnet and poem?

Lindy's decision to choose adoption for Noah, like
countless similar decisions by other birthmothers, was motivated by love: "I want the best for my child and I cannot
now give him that!" The hope for a better life is not the motivation of a person who does not care. Why, then, the first
myth?

We believe that the simple answer lies in the generally
held notion that one cannot be biologically responsible for
a child's life and make a logical decision not to parent that
child. Conceiving and then giving birth "naturally" mandates
at least eighteen years of daily parental responsibility, or so
we have been taught. To break this pattern by not assuming
the parental role is to be unnatural about something we hold
very dear—our families. Therefore, to protect the family unit
and the socially accepted order of things, birthmothers who
place their children in surrogate homes are conveniently
classified as unfeeling and uncaring—like fertile baby
machines.

Other influences also maintain the uncaring myth. Adoptive parents, coming from a perspective of imposed childlessness, find it especially difficult to understand the act of giving
away a baby. In addition, many individuals still believe that
bearing a child outside the sanctions of marriage is a shameful and unspeakable event. Their collective attitude toward
the birthmother ranges from superiority to condemnation to
punishment.

One birthmother still vividly remembers the emotional
aftermath of seeing her newborn son. After being with him
for about three hours, she returned her baby to the nurse
knowing that would be the last time she would see him. She

began to cry, "I cried all the tears that I will ever cry in my life in the hours after that. I cried long and hard." This birthmother asked then to see a minister, thinking that in some way he would be a comfort to her. The minister who responded to this tearful young woman proceeded to tell her what a terrible person she was. "You deserve the pain and agony you are feeling, and I am glad you realize that," he said.

In summary, believers of the first adoption myth label a birthmother as uncaring in order to explain her unnatural act, then justify condemning her by the righteous stance that, after all, nice girls would not do such things. If a nice girl would not or could not give away her child, then one may dismiss or punish this birthmother. One of the cruelest but most typical forms of punishment is forever denying the birthmother information about her child. "She does not deserve any information; she gave away all her rights," is the most common stance.

As you read the next letter, consider that this is a birthmother you may have heard about, or thought or spoken about in terms of the uncaring myth. Her letter, by contrast, reflects that the relinquishment of her son was accomplished only after careful and painstaking plans, not unthinking abandonment:

Dear Friends,

Another year has come and gone and Robert must be becoming a beautiful young man. At this hour exactly two years ago, joy came to my life and although you wouldn't know for several days, it also came to yours. Of course I always think of Robert and wish him well, but today especially, I am filled with warmth and love. I have read and heard of the longing and void most birth mothers feel on their child's birthday, and I must admit that I felt the same way last year at this time, but this year the feeling has blossomed to pride. It feels wonderful knowing that our son has experienced another year, and know that the new year holds growth and happiness not only for him, but for you.

It is a great coincidence that the time of Robert's birthday fell so near to the time of my reading of a book called *The Adoption Triangle*. It is a well put-together book, and I found it most interesting and informative. I read that most adoptive parents are only willing to accept healthy babies, whereas natural parents simply accept what they receive. Your wanting, accepting, and most importantly loving of Robert with the knowledge that he may have had a congenital disease really raises the respect that I feel for you. That is not the love adoptive parents give, but the love the *real* parents give.

I also read of the doubts and fears felt by birth parents, adoptees and adoptive parents. I guess that I am different because these are not the emotions which I have. I have always tried to express to you with openness, the loyalty and friendship which I have for you. I feel confident knowing that you will be open with Robert and that he can be honest with you. Don't ask me how I know, I just know. I do feel close to your family, and hope that you feel close to me.

The only new news that I have to relay is not of me, but of Robert's father, John. He and his wife are now expecting their second child. I do not know whether they are hoping for another boy or if they want a girl this time, but I do know that he will be happy with any child, and still be a wonderful father.

I must close for now, but not short of wishing your family all that's best and wishing Robert a very happy birthday.

Lovingly,

Lana

For us, the first myth of adoption is a troubling paradox. We know birthmothers like Lana relinquish their parental role and their legal rights because they want to give their child what they know he or she needs and what they think they cannot provide at that time—love, care, and security from two parents in a normal home situation. Yet these birthmothers who make careful and unselfish decisions are condemned and punished. Must they choose to raise their child themselves to avoid a lifetime of living with the first myth?

Birthmothers (especially teenagers) who experience an unplanned pregnancy are told by family members, social workers, and other adoption intermediaries about the wisdom of placing their child for adoption: "If you really loved your unborn child, you would make the responsible decision to place your child for adoption in a loving home with two parents." The entire counseling program for the birthmother when she is weighing her options emphasizes that if she chooses adoption she will be thinking, not of herself, but of "the welfare of her child."

Once legal relinquishment papers are signed, however, the same counselor may begin to practice behavior spelled out in the myth. The birthmother's responsible decision has somehow become "uncaring," an act of "abandonment," or a "failure as a person and as a parent." The paradox is emphasized every time post-placement counseling for the birthmother is brief or nonexistent, although the counseling during the decision-making process had been intense. This sudden switch in attitudes is viewed by the birthmother as a rejection of her and her decision, resulting in unnecessary confusion, unresolved feelings, and lingering doubts.

Our contact with birthmothers has dramatically convinced us that these women are not "unfeeling baby machines." A birthmother merely chooses to bring her child into this world, rather than abort it, and then to place that child in a home with two people who will nurture, guide, and assist the child to become an adult. As one birthmother wrote:

> . . . I had rather given Cara life than to go through with an abortion. The thought entered my mind that I could make a couple very happy. At the same time go on with my life. Also giving her a chance to live and grow up on God's Earth as a Human Being. And a beautiful one at that. Believe me it

would of hurt me worse if I'd had an abortion. So
instead I made four wonderful people happy, includ-
ing myself. . . .

Does this birthmother merit being labeled uncaring by
our society by participating in another act—the act of
abortion—which she dreads even more? Certainly we do not
believe she has earned the badge of an uncaring person
because she chose adoption as her best alternative. Nor
does this birthmother merit the punishment of forever being
denied simple information about her daughter. We think such
punishment far exceeds any possible crime.

Since we have rejected the fiction that birthmothers are
uncaring individuals, our work must deal with the depth and
variety of their emotions—emotions that remain long after
relinquishment papers are signed. Letters provide an avenue
for communication, as well as a familiar format that both
writer and receiver are comfortable using and handling.

Letter writing by birthmothers is helpful for them to come
to grips with their decision. Their letters serve as concrete
emotional outlets for feelings about the child's physical separation. By putting words on paper, a birthmother is forced
to focus on the reality of her decision. A letter may be her
best first step in healing and moving forward.

Tina, a nineteen-year-old birthmother, wrote her newborn son the day she was to leave the hospital. Tina had
cared for him throughout the hospital stay and her goodbye
to him is clearly painful:

My Dearest Son,
     It's so hard for me to start this letter. I have
so many things I would like to explain. But I am
not quite sure where to begin. I do want you to
remember that every decision I've made concerning you, was made out of love. And with only your
best interest at heart. I only hope that you realize
that my placing you for adoption doesn't mean I
don't love you Although it was hard for me to let
you go I know I made the right choice. Remember
I love you, I will always love and care for you.

Nothing will ever change that.

Let me first explain the relationship between your birthfather and me. I met your birthfather at a very vulnerable time in my life. You birthfather was also going thru rough times. We met one another when we needed each other the most. Together we loved and shared many special moments together. Sometimes during those special moments something beautiful happens. As did in our case. That something beautiful was you. But unfortunately the time we shared and the love we felt was only temporary. There wasn't enough to build a lifetime on. I wish things could have been different. But I don't regret what happened. I am so happy, so happy to have been apart of your creation.

When I looked at you, all the time we were in the hospital, I think you will look a lot like me. I really cannot see much of your birthfather in you right now. I am sure time will change all that. I do know that you were the most beautiful baby I had ever seen. From the moment you were born, you had such a wonderful color, such rosey chubby cheeks, and the cutest facial expressions I had ever seen. The whole time I spent with you, you were so good. Whenever I went to the nursery to see you all the other babies would be crying, but you were so content. You never cried or complained When it came time for your feeding and I would take you in my arms, you never seemed like you wanted to eat, just sleep. I am afraid you got your desire to sleep from me. I love to sleep.

Now because I am your birthmother, I wanted nothing but the best for you. I had to think of your life, separate from mine. I gave you life and in giving you life, I also had the responsibility of giving you the best life had to offer. I wanted you to have the best chance to live your life to the fullest. Even if that included living your life without me. That's why I chose adoption. Thru adoption I was able to make sure you had the things I couldn't

give you. You needed to be surrounded by the love
only a family can bring. To be in a home filled with
that love. To be brought up by two people who loved
each other, as much as they loved you. Alone I was
unable to give you all of this. Adoption is a gift
from my heart for you, Son. I wanted you to have
the world. I believe with all my heart you now have
it. Always remember how lucky you are. You have
two parents who love you just as much as I do. And
although you don't see me, I will always be with
you, my love for you continues everyday of my life.
I envy your parents, for they will be with you to
share all your ups and downs. But I thank God I
was able to have a part in your creation. I thank
Him for making it possible to share those first three
days with you. For there was never a moment you
were not loved. I will always have you in my
memories. With that memory goes my undying love.

I realize there's so little time and space to write
all the things I wanted to teach and explain to you.
I am glad I know your parents will be there to
answer and tell you everything you will need to
know about life. If I can I'd like to leave you with
a thought. I think if you listen and adhere to my
advice it will make life and the problems it brings
might be a little easier. Son, always <u>respect</u>
<u>yourself</u>, and show the same respect you show your-
self to every person you meet. Don't ever underesti-
mate yourself or put yourself down, always strive
to do the best you can, by all means you can! Everyone is bound to make mistakes. You find out what
went wrong and why. You learn from your mistakes,
then put it in the past, never dwell on them. Remember you're never alone. There's so many people stand-
ing on your side. Always ready and able to help,
should you need it. Together with love, you and your
family will overcome everything.

Today adoption records are kept closed to the
children that are placed for adoption. But even as
I write this letter, the laws are changing. I suspect

one day the records will be opened and you will be able to locate me. I will always welcome you with love and open arms. I'd like nothing better than to see you. But promise me the decision to find me will be your own. Don't ever let anyone, even me, pressure you into any decision you don't want to make. As long as you're happy, I will be happy. I will understand and accept any decision you make.

Forever, you will remain a part of me. I will always be proud of you, Son. My love always with you.

I pray nothing but good times fill your days and nights.

Good luck in whatever you do.

Always,
With All My Love,
Your Birth Mother
Tina

Tina's letter is the farewell to her son that is needed for her to begin to fully understand and accept his life separate from hers. Without the letter, Tina might be forced to deal with her son's placement in any of a number of vastly different ways. One birthmother who was denied this type of communication and post-placement support, recalled many years later (at age thirty-five), "After I signed the papers, I hated myself. I started hanging around with people involved in heavy drinking and drugs. I felt like I deserved that. I believe I would be dead or crazy now, if I did not get pregnant and keep my second child." This mother was consumed by a need to punish herself for her uncaring act, and to redo her decision. Sadly, we know many other birthmothers who relate similar dramatic stories that emphasize how their adoption decision traumatizes them for a lifetime.

Tina, by contrast, was allowed to deal with her decision and her loss by communicating her love to her son. Her feelings were not discounted by the counselors who had worked with her, and she was not subtly rejected. Tina was helped to go on with her life without the guilt and pain caused by the myth's sudden condemnation.

Letter exchanges also benefit others in the adoption drama. Adoptive parents are given a unique opportunity to know the birthmother of their child from personal correspondence. This helps erase shadowy stereotypes of those "other parents" that might affect their relationship with their child. Adoptive parents also receive direct information and facts to share with their children rather than innuendo and guesswork when the inevitable questions come. One adoptive mother told us, "I treasure the letters to my sons. They let me off the hook of having the total responsibility of teaching the boys that their birthparents were real people with regular feelings, hopes, and pain."

Adoptees also benefit from the rejection of the first myth through the letter exchanges. In a personal letter, the central question of every adoptee, "How could someone give me away?" is answered by the only person capable of providing an answer. Tina's son, for example, will not be forced to internalize feelings of worthlessness from having been "discarded." Regrettably, much of the pain other adoptees experience will not be lessened. Society's tenacious belief in the first myth will always translate for them as "obviously your birthmother did not and does not care about you."

In order that our rejection of the first myth become more than a hollow protest against a social ill, we have taken steps to change the public's belief in this myth. Foremost among these steps is the letter exchanges which we encourage. Here is a recap of what we are convinced the letters accomplish:

• For birthmothers, letters constructively focus feelings of love and loss.
• For adoptive parents, letters awaken needed empathy and insight.
• For the adoptee, letters answer questions positively.

We hope that the few letters we have shared so far with you, our reader, have encouraged you to question and reject ready assumptions that birthmothers "obviously do not care."

2
Lifting
the Veil of Secrecy

Myth Number Two:
*"Secrecy in every phase of the adoption
process is necessary to protect
all parties."*

Secrecy in adoption proceedings continues as today's most persistently practiced myth. Widespread support for anonymity between the participants in adoption remains unquestioned by many adoption agencies, other professional intermediaries, and society in general. In both traditional and semi-open adoption, full identities of the parties involved are not shared. In fairness to the supporters of secrecy, their motivation stems from the desire to protect the adoptive parents, the birthparents, and the child. We are convinced that this desire is misguided.

Adoption was not always a matter of secrecy, nor did laws always seal adoption records. In Colonial days, adoption could be accomplished by merely recording the transfer of a child, much like we now transfer the deed to our homes or title to our cars. Early laws, such as those passed in Texas and Vermont in 1850, were intended to make this type of informal adoption more secure. All court records, however, were open to the public.

The origin of the second myth of adoption and the practice of sealing records has to be understood in the light of a different era, the early 1900's. Social work as a profession was just developing. Unlike today, there were many destitute children available for adoption, but few potential adoptive parents. It was largely believed that such social ills as poverty, sexual promiscuity, alcoholism, and crime were passed on to children in the genes. For that reason middle-class family members feared taking to their hearts a child of questionable parentage. The risk was just too great that the maturing child would exhibit the sinful attributes of the criminal or perverted parents.

In order to sell the public on adoption as a viable means of caring for large numbers of children, social workers needed to establish themselves as experts in matching children to families. They thus assumed the status of a third party between prospective adoptive parents and birthparents. The pressures of trying to recruit adoptive parents led social workers to give assurances that the child was without physical, emotional, or mental defect.

The selling job that this profession mounted involved legislative protection as an essential element. Sealed records evolved, in effect concealing the background of the child. In addition, the child's birth certificate no longer was stamped with the fact of illegitimate birth. Later, replacement birth certificates began to be issued, listing names of the adoptive parents as if the child had been naturally born to them. This practice of issuing new birth certificates was termed a "legal rebirth" for the adoptee. What started as a process to make adoption more attractive and to protect the child from being forever haunted by his illegitimate birth became linked with the idea of rebirth and the mandate of secrecy. By 1950 most states had laws forever sealing original birth certificates and court records, not only from the public but also from the adoptive parents and the adoptee.

Today, adoptive parents in traditional or semi-open adoptions receive selected information both about the child they plan to adopt and about the individuals who gave him life. Selection is made by social workers and other adoption intermediaries who decide which facts to share and which facts are best left secret. This sifting of information invariably weeds out certain factors. Rarely do adoptive parents obtain detailed social histories on both birthparents or their immediate families. Medical histories are provided, but the information revealed is sometimes only oral. Even when written medical histories are provided, adoptive parents must remember that the child's medical background is not "complete," since one's medical history continues to evolve over time. In addition, social realities of the birthparents such as alcohol or drug usage are frequently omitted. One adoption social worker we know believes that the adoptive couple needs "only the positives." This social worker has identified herself with numerous individuals who, possibly unconsciously, harbor the belief that adoptive parents are doing the homeless child a favor. Therefore we still hear, "How wonderful of you to adopt that poor baby!" as if the couple is being courageous and generous.

Secrecy imposed on adoptive parents is also motivated by a desire to protect the infertile couple denied their own natural child. The conventional wisdom of the professional in control of the adoption proceedings is, "The adoptive couple will be happiest if they can be as much like natural parents as possible." This translates to providing the couple with a near-perfect child, securing the same legal status as "real parents," and then helping them forget the different way their family unit was formed. Forgetting is encouraged every time the professional in control decides not to mention the role birthparents may play in the adoptee's future or the unique responsibilities of adoptive parenthood. Some physical likeness between the child and his adoptive parents will help dispel any questions about his origins, and the adoptive parents will be further protected from publicly facing the reality of their childlessness.

Birthparents are also supposedly protected by secrecy of traditional adoption practices. They are essentially told by the professional intermediary, "Give us the baby you have decided to place. Now you can go away and forget this experience; we will protect you." Such protection includes withholding information from them about the adoptive family's physical appearance, interests, or personalities. By denying specific facts about the people who will nurture and guide the adoptee to adulthood, the intermediary assumes birthparents live easier with their decision. Their logic represents the "out of sight, out of mind" philosophy. If the intermediary is progressive and compassionate, birthparents might receive a brief, probably oral, profile of the adoptive family. Interestingly, the adoptive family is almost always described as a "professional family who is financially stable and will provide a loving home."

Finally, the second myth of adoption is designed to protect the adoptee. Although illegitimacy lacks its past shameful connotations, and attitudes toward bringing children of different or "bad" blood into the family are not as prevalent, many individuals believe that secrecy is necessary to hide socially abhorrent elements in the child's background. The goal is to shield the adoptee from the unfavorable information in his own birth history.

Similarly, secrecy in all phases of adoptive practices is used to spare the child the conflict of two sets of parents. The logic here stems from the idea that believing something makes it true. Deny the fact that two caring birthparents exist and they will not exist, especially if the adoptive parents do a good job at parenting. In total, the personal wisdom and persistent mythology of the social worker or other professional intermediary controls the adoptee's future—"some facts are best concealed so that the adoptee-child will be forever protected."

The adoption practices described above result directly from an adherence to the second myth. When we began to question the basis of these practices, we uncovered numerous problems. We discovered that there exist latent messages in the intermediary's selection of information and encouraged forgetting. These messages serve to harm, not protect, the individuals involved in the adoption drama. Adoptive parents, birthparents, and adoptees are actually forced to cope, without recourse or review, with what the intermediary thought was in their best interest.

For adoptive parents, secrecy handicaps their parental role identification. Because the adoptive parents typically are not provided much information about the individuals who gave their child life, birthparents remain shadowy stereotypes. The intermediary message to be as much like natural parents as possible also translates to mean that adoptive parenthood must be second best to the status of a "real parent."

Birthparents are also seriously encumbered by closed adoption. Denial of information about the adoptive parents prevents them from ever being sure that their decision was right. "Do the adoptive parents love him as much as I do? Is he safe and protected? Is he healthy and happy?" The questions persist for millions of birthparents, but the questions remain unanswered. In addition, the message to the birthparent from the trained intermediary to "try not to think about it" translates to impose a lifetime of shame, for "it" must be a shameful mistake or an unforgivable sin.

Finally, secrecy robs the adoptee of his right to reach his full potential. Instead of his psychological energy being directed to the normal process of growth, the adoptee spends time dwelling on the unanswered questions, "Who are my birthparents?" and "Why am I not with them?"

As with the first myth of adoption, we reject the need for secrecy between members of the adoption drama. Imposed secrecy denies individual choice and robs human potential. It prevents honesty and forces a punitive distance among the five people fate brought together.

Once again, we use letters to bridge the chasm traditionally created by mandatory anonymity. Letters move all participants expectantly toward the benefits only possible through honest and open sharing:

Dear Birthmother,

I am writing a letter I have wanted to write for three years now. The child you gave birth to just over three years ago is my daughter—Stacy.

The reason I have wanted to write you is because I want you to know that the child you created, nurtured for nine months, gave birth to, and then placed with me is very special. When I look at her beautiful face I think of you and know you must be beautiful. When I am enjoying her gentle, loving nature, I think of you and know you must be gentle. When I get somewhat frightened by her intelligence, I think of you and know you must be bright.

Always know that I am fully aware of the

magnitude of the gift you placed with us. I am committed to Stacy growing up to be a secure and happy woman. I thank you for letting me parent her. I am comfortable as Stacy's mother and I am willing to share with you letters about and pictures of our daughter if and when you would like these.

I have written this letter as one mother to another. My husband is also committed to the offer of communication and certainly to our daughter.

I will write again if you wish. If not, that is okay.

Stacy is well and happy and will grow up a secure and wonderful person.

Love,
Stacy's Mom

The preceding letter was written by Stacy's adoptive mother three years after her adoption. At the time Stacy was adopted, letters were infrequently exchanged because we were still deluded by the second myth. Stacy's adoptive mother, however, felt a strong need to communicate her feelings. "I have needed to tell my child's birthmother these things for a long time," she said. "I'm just glad I could." The letter was delivered by the adoption agency to Stacy's birthmother who eagerly received such unexpected communication. To date Stacy's birthmother has not written a return letter but the bridge for future communication was opened.

Today many adoption intermediaries encourage the exchange of letters and pictures between adoptive parents, birthparents, and their children (and in open adoptions, the exchange of full identifying information and the access to ongoing contact over the years). Picture exchanges include current photographs of the children, the birthparents, and the adoptive parents. Several years ago, most adoption professionals would have never considered such exchanges. We believed secrecy and total anonymity were necessary. Shattering this second myth was more difficult for us than the first because all our training had taught us that our closed methods really did protect our clients. Our belief in this new approach grew stronger, however, with the repeated and sincere excitement of our clients as they received personal information, names, and pictures. Instead of our openness having a chilling effect on the participants in our adoption stories, they began to demand even more openness and less protective measures. Today our parents seem to accept these exchanges as basic to the adoption process.

Denise, a twenty-seven-year-old adoptive mother, describes in the following letter why she does not want a veil of secrecy between her and her son's birthmother:

To a very special person,

I am writing this letter to a person who has a special place in my heart. You have given me something so precious and special—my son. He is the greatest joy in my life.

This letter is very difficult to write—not because I don't want to—but because I don't have a name to identify you with. What little bit I do know about you makes me feel like we're a lot alike. We seem to have similar interests in hobbies. Even though we've never met I consider you a special type of friend.

We have named our son James. He has to be the most beautiful baby in the world. His features are so perfect. Of course, he is growing in leaps and bounds. All of his baby hair has fallen out and new hair is growing in. I think his hair is going to be brown to match his beautiful <u>huge</u> brown eyes.

I'm not sure if great detail is what you would like to read or not so I'm playing this by ear—here goes.

James is very active and alert. He has been turning from his stomach to back for about two weeks now. It won't be long before he will be sitting alone and crawling. He gets so frustrated when he can't do something but he is persistent. To date, James doesn't have any teeth but he sure is drooling a lot (has been for about 2 months). Ever since James came to us he has been trying to suck his thumb but never could figure out how to hold onto it. Well, he has figured out how and is an avid thumb sucker. I tried to give him a pacifier but he acted like it was choking him. The only time he really sucks his thumb is when he is tired or sleepy. James' sleeping habits are great—he goes to bed (by his choice) at 8:30 P.M. and sleeps until 9 or 10 A.M. He really likes and requires a lot of sleep. James is definitely a little creature of habit, he doesn't take too well to his routine being disrupted. Right now he is going through a stage where he cries at the mere sight of a stranger (even his grandparents). I've been told this is very normal and that he will outgrow it. James tends to be on the serious side. He always looks as if he is in deep thought. He is not very generous with his smiles yet, but when he does smile it's worth the wait. It looks as though he is going to be rather cautious of people until he knows them well—that's good in a way.

I could ramble on for hours but I'm not sure that's a good idea. I feel like you loved James very much and I don't want to cause you any unnecessary pain. I love James more than words on paper can begin to describe. He gives me so much pleasure and has brought joy to everyone in our family. Without you I would not be experiencing such joy and for that I am very grateful to you. I know you will never forget James but I hope you will never worry about him. James has a very loving family and will always be taken care of. I saved all of the background information concerning yourself and James' birthfather. When James is old enough I will give it to him. It is my sincere hope that someday you will feel comfortable in writing James a letter. It will be kept with everything else and given to him later on. If James wishes to locate you when he is of age, I have promised myself to help him in anyway I can. I hope you will be receptive if that search ever takes place.

For now you should concentrate on your future. I know it will be bright and happy. Please remember

that you will always have two anonymous friends
who think you are very special. You gave joy to
me and my husband by giving life to our son. We
will always be grateful.

> God Bless You,
> Denise

All members of the adoption drama benefit from lifting
the veil of secrecy. Adoptive parents are not denied information about the individuals who gave their child life. Stereotypes of the child's birthparents are replaced with actual facts
and personal data about the birthmother and birthfather.
Through individual communication via the letter exchanges,
adoptive parents learn about and empathize with the birthparents. The insight that develops will be invaluable to the
adoptee as he begins to question his adoptive parents about
his heritage and his birthparents.

Paula and Ken are adoptive parents who were married
four years before they sought adoption to form the family they
wanted. They began adoption proceedings believing birthmothers were probably uncaring and birthfathers irresponsible. They subsequently learned from their birthmother that
neither of these half-formed stereotypes was true. Three
months after they brought their son Michael home, they wrote
his birthmother the following letter. Consider how Michael will
benefit when he asks his Mom and Dad, "Where did I come
from?" or "Who are my birthparents?"

To Michael's Birthmother,

Well, where do I begin to tell you how happy
Michael has made us? First let me tell you my name
is Paula and my husband's name is Ken. We would
be happy for you to share your first name with us
if you feel comfortable doing so.

I'll start by telling you a little about Michael.
He weighs about 14 pounds and is about 25 inches
long. He does not have much hair yet so you cannot
really tell what color it is going to be. His eyes were
blue-gray but are gradually turning lighter blue.
He was baptized on March 8. We take him to church

most Sundays. He usually sleeps right through the service, which is sure nice. Even if he is awake, he rarely fusses during the service.

He is a very good baby—he has never cried very much. He is a happy baby—always smiling and "talking." He charms everybody he meets.

He has a bit of a temper when he doesn't get his way. But then, don't we all? He is a very strong baby. He can already creep around when I lay him on his stomach.

Michael has been a very special addition to our family. Since Ken and I cannot have biological children, Michael was a dream come true. Your sacrifice was our gain and we truly appreciate your difficult decision. He is the first grandchild in both families and the first great grandchild on my side of the family. He is loved (and spoiled) by every member of our families.

Now let me try to express our feelings, about you, Michael, and the entire adoption. Please bear with me because I am not very good at writing my feelings down on paper. We really admire you for making the difficult decision that you had to make. You put your own desires aside and thought about what the baby needed. We know this was not an easy thing to do. I will be honest with you and say that had I been in your shoes with this decision to make, I am not sure I could have been as unselfish as you have been. We know that you will never forget Michael and that he will always have a special place in your heart. We hope when you think of him you will be happy because you know he is in a good home with people who love him very much. When I reread that last sentence it occurred to me that you may never really be happy about this decision, but we at least hope you can be at peace with yourself knowing he has loving parents and a good home. I know that the agency has an excellent program for the birth mothers and we are confident that this has helped you handle all the different emotions you must be feeling now.

Sometimes we look at Michael and we have a hard time believing he is really ours. But, because of you he is ours and we can never thank you enough. May God bless you and be with you always.

Paula and Ken

We think Michael's sense of identity can only be strengthened by the love shared between his collective parents.

Adoptive parents benefit in a second powerful way when secrecy disappears. They are able to accept the dignity of their role as adoptive parents. This includes understanding and accepting this role and its realities without feeling second-best to the child's birthparents. There is no subtle message from an influential intermediary that they must fear and compete with the child's "real parents."

The adoptive mother who wrote this next letter has accepted her role as mother to two children who were not born to her. Her role in the life of her children is different from that role either birthmother will have. Different, however, does not mean substitute or second-best. She is simply a mother who loves her children very much:

Dear Birthmother,

I just wanted to let you know how much we are enjoying our new son. We feel so fortunate to have him to love and raise. He has been accepted with joy by all of his new family—grandmas and grandpas, aunts and uncles, and especially by his new dad, mom, and big sister. Our daughter loves to dance and sing for her new brother and to show him off to her friends. And, of course, the baby loves to watch his sister and be with her!

His new dad enjoys talking to our baby about the adventures they will have together when he's old enough to play ball, fish, and hunt! We're all looking forward to camping together this summer.

I thought you'd like to know what a happy and healthy baby our new little one is. He eats well, sleeps well, and loves to "talk" and smile with us. He is such a good baby!

We want you to know that we very much respect the difficult decision you have had to make. You will always have a special place in our hearts for the love that you have felt for our little son. We wish you every happiness in the future. We will make sure that the baby gets the letter you wrote to him when he is old enough to understand. We want him to know how much you cared for him and why he was placed for adoption, and to feel good about himself. We also want him to be happy with his heritage—biological and adoptive—and we try to incorporate traditions which include all of the backgrounds of the people in our very special family. We are happy for our daughter and our new son that they are both adopted. This will be a good thing for them to share. They can help each other to accept the fact that they were adopted. But, please know that we could never love any child any more than we do our two precious children. They are a dream come true for us and always will be.

We wish you health, happiness, and peace.

Sincerely,

Ann

Birthparents also benefit without the imposed secrecy of the second myth. Through the communication opened by the letter exchanges, birthparents learn about the people parenting their child. This information is essential for them to find peace with their adoption decision.

Ralph and Diane, a young married couple, felt unable to parent their first child. They represent the minority of birthparents—those who are married and still choose adoptive placement. It is perhaps harder for society to accept the idea of a married couple placing a child for adoption. So, traditionally, there has been even more of a tendency to place the child veiled in secrecy. Ralph and Diane rejected this mode of placement. While they felt emotionally unprepared for parenthood, they also loved their newborn daughter and had certain specifications for the type of family and environment they wanted for her. In a lengthy letter to the adoptive parents they chose, Ralph and Diane communicated their wishes and their love to their daughter, Jessica, and to her "new" parents. In this fragment from their letter, both pain and generosity come clearly to all of us:

> God really did mean for her to be your baby
> and for you to raise her as your own.

Ralph and Diane will never forget Jessica, but they can take solace in Jessica's growing up in an environment and home they chose. Secrecy for this couple, as for most birthparents, would have taken away the social support necessary for their process of grieving. They would have been told to forget rather than encouraged to feel and share their love with their daughter and her adoptive parents.

Shattering the secrecy myth also allows birthparents to feel good about themselves because adoptive parents are consistently supportive of the birthparents, and their letters reflect this encouragement. For the birthparents this opportunity to take pride in their responsible act of adoption is a unique experience. Such encouragement frees birthparents of the guilt and shame so commonly imposed in the past.

Consider how reinforced Colleen must have felt about her decision to place her son, Jed, for adoption after she received the following letter:

> Dear Colleen,
>
> First, an apology for such a long delay between receiving your letter and Jed's giraffe and this response from us. I'm typing so I can get my thoughts down as fast as they come. We have so very much to share with you! The picture you sent is beautiful, one we will treasure and look forward to sharing with Jed. He favors you in so many features as you will be able to see from the pictures we are enclosing.
>
> We have truly been blessed with not only a beautiful little boy but such a good baby. He has

been sleeping through the night since Christmas Day! The other night he surprised us by sleeping a long eleven-hour night. The whole family enjoyed that! He has a really happy disposition—loves people and watches everything that goes on around him. When he was just three weeks old we took him to Portland, Maine, for Thanksgiving. It was a long flight and a few plane changes but he fared very well and, even at that young age, watched everything and everyone around. We think he is unusually bright, of course!

At the first visit to the Pediatrician Jed had gained to 10 lbs. and stretched out 1/2 in. He is up to about 12 lbs. now. Since five weeks he has been taking cereal and adding something else new each week. What an eater he is?! Loves bananas (his favorite), squash, applesauce, pears, sweet potatoes (green beans just so-so). We have decided this week that his appetite now parallels the dog's and she is 45 lbs.! He isn't fat but he really is stretching out and growing out of his clothes. (Wears large 3 mos. or small 6 mos. sizes now!)

Jed has been holding his head up strongly since 2 months and follows voices now. Just yesterday Carl watched him turn over for the first time from his tummy to his back and a repeat performance. I was away for the afternoon and missed all the excitement. You must think I am very biased and not sharing anything negative with you. Jed does have a temper but the neat part about it—he usually has a valid complaint and either way he is so easy to console! We both admire that quality in him. No hair! Well, maybe just a little. . . . When the sun shines just right across his "hair" it looks red-blonde to me and his eyelashes are also the same color. He will be a real heart-breaker with his big blue eyes! He has a most charming pug nose (so do I) and a full face that truly lights up when he smiles.

We left Christmas Day to spend the holiday up North with both of our families. Jed seemed to do pretty well with all the long travel hours, many airports and airplanes and long drives. The relatives just loved him! Both of our parents felt so much emotion for him and had a hard time letting us take him back home. My parents are looking forward to going to Colorado with us next month and watching Jed during the day while we go skiing. Don't think they have ski sizes to fit Jed—otherwise he would probably want to try it!

Some of Jed's favorite things: watching football games, eating, eating, taking long naps, loves his bath!, getting all dressed up and looking in the mirror, being rocked to sleep, riding in the car listening to soothing music. The list seems to go on and on. . . .

I have shared all I can think of for now, Carl will think of some things I forgot.

. . . We respect your feelings and want only the things that will help you through this most difficult time in your life. We think of you each day as we look at our beautiful son and we pray for you that the growing that you are doing will be richly blessed. Your decision to carry and nurture Jed so that he could experience life will carry many blessings for you throughout your life. I am convinced of that. Each time I look at him and realize that had someone else conceived him, they may have chosen abortion as an alternate and he would never have been, I thank God he was entrusted to you and now has been brought into our lives.

I look forward to meeting you one day!

> With love for you always,
> Sandy

The love and gratitude in the above letter release Colleen from any need to live a lifetime feeling guilty about her decision. Colleen, as with many of our birthmothers, has received the social support necessary to parent future children, continue her education, or advance professionally.

Frequently, letters deeply reflect all the sincere gratitude and love felt. Letters also do not simply sing general praises, but become very specific, very personal, and very memorable for the details of human sharing. Here is but one such example:

Dear Parents of My Little Angel,

I deeply appreciate your thoughtfulness and concern for my well-being. I would also like to thank you for sharing with me the joy and happiness you've found in her. One of my main concerns for her was that I wanted her to be well loved by one and all, and you have done just that. I'm also very happy to know that you plan to make her bilingual, since I myself am bilingual. I know of the advantages of being bilingual. Oh, I can go on and on with <u>Thanks</u> to you, for all you have done and will continue to do for her. I can't find the words to express the happiness and relief that I feel. When I first put her for adoption, I thought that I would feel regret for my actions and that she wouldn't be well taken care of. But the more I hear about her wonderful parents, the less I worry about her. And now I'm positive that she will get all that I ever wanted for her.

Thank-you always,
Your daughter's
birth mother

P.S. These earrings, that I want my Little Angel to have, have a special meaning behind them. You see, when I was born, my grandmother went out and bought them for me since I was the first (and only) girl in the family. But since I never got my ears pierced, I wanted her to have them.

I also want her to have this blanket that I crocheted for her. I wanted her to have something that I made. I couldn't decide on what to make at first but once I decided, I got excited and had it made quicker than I expected. Again, <u>Thank-You</u> for wanting my Li'l Angel and for just being You.

The final member in the adoption drama to benefit from the rejection of the second myth is the adoptee. He benefits because his collective parents are permitted to grow secure in their particular roles in his life. His adoptive parents are not unwittingly encouraged to compete to possess him. Nor are his birthparents punished and banished from a place in his life. The adoptee can feel good about the individuals who "together" give him life. He also receives the rare treasure of a personal and truly meaningful letter that he would otherwise be denied.

To My Little Angel,

A precious, innocent and beautiful child who I have Loved from the moment I was first aware of her presence inside me. I will always love you, care about you, worry about you and wonder how much you've grown and how your life has turned out to be. My sweet child, you were created out of Love, a love that your biological father and I shared for a couple of years. We were both young, with changes in our own individual lives; changes that were hard for the other to understand and accept, which caused our life together to fall apart. I guess it was time for us to go our separate ways, to be free to experience and be aware of ourselves as individuals. Giving you up for adoption was one of the hardest decisions I ever had to make. I wanted to keep you, to tell everyone that you were mine, to provide everything and more for you and be so very proud. But you see, I had to face the fact that it would have made both of our lives extremely difficult. I wanted you to have the same kind of childhood that I had. Growing up in a family with a set of parents who cared enough to provide the very best of everything. Which was something I could not give you unless I worked at two jobs while I was also trying to continue college. I couldn't see myself leaving you with someone while I worked day and night with no time for you. Depriving you of the love and attention you so desperately need from a set of full time parents.

So once I decided on adoption, I felt good about my decision and knew it was for the best. We both have a lifetime ahead of us and I know that your parents will make it a happy one for you. I've heard nothing but positive things about them and I couldn't have picked a better set of parents for you myself. As for my life, I will pick up the pieces and make the best of my road to the future.

I've heard people talk against adoption, but they don't see all the aspects and advantages in it. They say that I've lost you forever, but no matter what the circumstances, I see it as "no matter what anyone says, you will always be my child in my heart, only that somewhere on this earth, there is a wonderful couple taking care of you."

Sincerely,
Your birthmother

3

Birthparents
Remember Forever

Myth Number Three:
*Both the birthmother and birthfather
will forget about their unwanted child.*

The third typical myth endures despite all available information that distinctly proclaims that birthparents remember their birthchild for a lifetime. The most frequent and persuasive source of this information remains the birthparents themselves. As a group, these men and women have circulated expressive and clear statements. Here is an example, from a brochure produced by Concerned United Birthparents, Inc.:

> ... A birthparent's feelings are not automatically obliterated upon affixing a signature to a contract; however much of society has been led to believe that. Many, perhaps most endure another pain: a "lifelong sense of psychological amputation," wondering if their birthchild is well and happy or even alive! This unique pain defies description.

Our own experiences support that sensitive CUB statement. No birthmother we have ever known has ever forgotten that little life that was so much a part of her for nine months. Nor have we met a birthfather who easily dismisses the fact he has fathered a child. Mary, an eighteen-year-old birthmother, tells us that after three years she still thinks of her blue-eyed daughter with the love evident in this, her first letter, written seven weeks after her daughter was born:

Dear Daughter,

I've read the social history of your family over and over, and I believe that you will now be able to have the kind of life that I want you to have. Although it was very hard for me to give you up, I feel that it is best for you to have a stable family that will be able to give you all the time and things that you will need.

Your birthfather and I came to Texas from up north. We both love the ocean and being outdoors. I hope that you will have the chance to go to the ocean with your family, and living in the country, I hope you will get to be outside as much as you want.

Your birthfather is a very warm, sensitive person who was with me all through my pregnancy and hospital stay. We care about each other, but we both have a lot of growing and learning to do before we even consider making a lifelong commitment.

When I found out that I was pregnant, many things went through my mind, but I always tried to keep in mind what was best for you. I feel that it is important for you to have a mother and father who not only love you, but are stable in their relationship as well. Our financial condition was another consideration, as it would have been very hard just to buy all the things you would need, and things that you would have wanted would be almost impossible to buy. I also feel that it is important for a family to spend time together, and as I plan on going to college and working, I would not have been able to spend the time with you that I feel is important.

Your birthfather and I love you very much. I hope you will understand that it is because we love you so much that you are now a member of a very special family; ready to give you all the time, attention, love and anything else you may need.

After you were born, I realized how hard it would be to say good-bye to you. You were such a beautiful baby. I could always pick you out in the nursery; you didn't have much hair (that helped me pick you out!), but you were also very special-looking, your eyes were such a be<u>autif</u>ul blue, and you were such a good baby. The nurses brought you to me to feed, and each time they brought you, it got harder, and I would cry all over you, and I know that although it was the hardest thing I have ever done, it was the right decision. Your family loves you very much and they will be able to give you all the love, time and special attention that I want you to have.

I always wanted to have a big brother (I have two little brothers) and I hope you will feel lucky to have one.

It's taken me almost seven weeks to write this letter but it's taken me that long to really believe that it was really the right decision. If you ever feel discouraged, always remember that your family wanted you very much, and because we all love you, your birthfather and I, you are now a very special member of a very special family.

All my love,
Your Birthmother

Information disseminated by the Concerned United Birthparent group in the publication "The Birthparent Perspective" also addresses a frequent corollary to the forgetting myth:

If the birthparents have gone on with their lives and have forgotten, then the social worker, adoption intermediary, and judge must protect their privacy over the adult adoptee's desire to seek a reunion.

This comment and its protective attitude is soundly rejected by most birthparents. Very few want anonymity. Besides which, they rightfully remind powerful individuals in control that they have a right to be asked, before their privacy is automatically protected and their child is denied access to them. As Concerned United Birthparents, Inc., writes in their widely circulated pamphlet:

> Adoptees have the absolute right to full and accurate information about their origins, including identification of, and meeting with, the birthparents, whenever and whatever age there is a need. . . . Our experience—and researchers and activist groups who effect reunions agree— shows that only a scant minority want anonymity. . . . Most birthparents are overjoyed to finally know the fate of their birthchild, and to close a long, painful chapter of wondering.*

Susan, a thirty-four year old birthmother, writes of her long need to someday meet her daughter (whom she had also named Susan). This letter was written fourteen years after her daughter's placement:

Dear Susan,

That's the name I gave you when you were born but I'm sure you're parents have renamed you.

There are so many things that I would like to say to you and so much of my life that I really want to share with you. I'm sure I could never begin to come close in a letter.

Until recently I didn't know that it was possible to write you a letter and that you might someday read it and find out that I did love you very much when you were born. I love you very much now and have loved you all these years. Every June on your birthday you are remembered and I say a special prayer for you often.

If you should ever wish to find me, it shouldn't be too hard. Right now I live in San Antonio but won't put the address in here as we are going to

---

*Concerned United Birthparents, Inc., *The Birthparents' Perspective*, (pamphlet), Milford, MA, (undated).

be moving to another house soon. We both like San Antonio and plan to stay here for awhile.

As I said at the beginning of this letter, I want to share so very much with you and I wish you could share all of your life with. . . . There are so many relatives you could claim I don't know where to start telling you about them. Maybe that would be best left until we meet. Both sets of my grandparents are still living at this time, along with all of my Aunts and Uncles and their children. Not to mention a lot of them on Martin's side of the family.

I am enclosing a picture of Martin and our two children taken last year. They haven't changed too much since then but probably will have by the time you read this. Also enclosed is a picture taken about a year after Martin and I were married. It is from my grandparents 50th wedding anniversary party. It is not too clear but you can get an idea of what everyone looks like. These are my brother and my sisters and myself along with our grandparents— my mother's father and mother.

Well, Susan, I guess you can tell I'm excited about telling you things but I guess I had better close this letter and hope that someday you will want to know more.

If you ever want, need or desire to know me and the rest of your family, we are all here and I am waiting.

You should not take any of this to mean that I ever want to interfere with your life or take any love away from your parents. To me they are very special people and maybe someday they will know from me how much I think of them too.

Only you and they know what it would mean if you try to find me. Don't ever do anything to hurt them because they are your parents.

All my love always,
Your Susan

The myth that birthparents forget persists in spite of clear evidence to the contrary. Such an error is not just the result of folk tales and gossip. This apparent contradiction in logic results very much from the rationalization of adoption intermediaries, families, friends, and adoptive parents. These four powerful influences maintain the myth because of their own need to believe it is true.

For the adoption intermediary to acknowledge that birthparents have lifetime feelings, especially sorrow, about the placement of a child is to recognize the extensive therapy and post-adoption counseling birthparents require. This assistance, of course, consumes time and dollars of the adoption agency and professional intermediary. How much easier to rationalize away the aftermath of adoption, rather than to develop a program to treat the effects of a "psychological amputation." Therefore, the intermediary tends to cling to the belief that the birthparents quickly dismiss their adoption experience and their child. Only this belief permits the professional guilt-free termination of contact after the birth of the child and after the relinquishment papers are signed.

For the family member of a birthparent, loss of a child through adoption compares to the loss of a child through death. Interestingly, while family members are assisted in their grief over the death of a family member, rarely does society condone the same grief when a family member is lost because of an adoptive placement. Yet, for some, the placement of a child might mean the loss of a grandchild they will never know.

The following letter was written to Marsha's birthson whom she placed for adoption at one week. Marsha speaks of the involvement of her birthson's grandmother. Although her letter does not indicate this, Marsha's mother said goodbye to her first and only grandchild in the few minutes she held him close:

Dear Son,
    First of all I want you to know that I love you very much and I always will. I'm writing this letter to let you know why I put you up for adoption.

It wasn't an easy decision but I was thinking of you and your life. I wanted you to have the best life possible. I was in a position where I couldn't make that happen. Let me explain the situation between your father and I. We didn't know each other very long before I became pregnant. But we did care for each other very much. We were both young and we weren't ready to raise a baby the way it should be done. Your father didn't earn enough money for all three of us much less himself. We didn't want you to have a hard time growing up. We wanted you to be happy. I hope you can understand that I was only thinking of what was best for you.

I didn't want to give you up but I did it out of love for you. I really wish it had been different and I'm sorry it wasn't.

I thought it would be nice if you knew a little about your grandparents. When I was pregnant with you they made sure I took good care of myself and you. Your grandmother especially made sure I took care so that you would come out to be the beautiful and healthy little baby you were. They wanted you to have a good home and be happy too. When we were in the hospital they came to visit everyday. That first time I saw you was a very special day. When I got to hold you for the first time you were sleeping peacefully in my arms. I didn't want to let you go. I wanted to hold you forever. I will never forget that day. Your grandmother held you next. She looked so happy and said you were a beautiful baby. You hardly cried at all, you were a good baby. You had a beautiful smile. I even got to feed you and that also was a special time for me. You ate so well that I knew you were going to grow up strong and healthy.

I thought I would let you know that I had a name for you. It's Mitchell. I will always treasure those moments I had with you. I hope that where ever you are, you're happy. I will always be

wondering where you are and what you're doing.
Please take care, son. I love you so very much.
                    Love Always,
                    Your Birthmother

Grandparents like Marsha's mother do miss their grandchild. Their mourning, however, is done in silence. They too
want to believe their own children forget because that frees
them from dwelling on their own pain and possible guilt at
their inability to do more to prevent "their own loss."

For other family members the need to believe that the
birthparents forget is the easiest way to deny the experience.
Peggy's father would not deal with his sixteen-year-old's
unwed pregnancy. When Peggy wrote her birthson the following letter, both her pain and her family's pain were made
obvious. Peggy's father will continue to believe that both
Peggy and her mother will forget because he desperately
wants the painful topic to be honorably closed:

Dear Son,
    I am writing this letter to you in hope that
you may understand why I had to have you adopted.
    I am 19 years old and the only daughter of
four. I have one brother older than I and two youn-
ger than I. My father has always thought of me
as his little girl. I guess he always will.
    I was sixteen when I became pregnant with
you. Both my parents were hurt. Since I don't believe
in abortion, I decided to go ahead and have you.
I wanted to keep you so very much.
    But not being married, my father thought it
best I have you adopted. It broke my heart to have
to give you away. My mother wanted you as much
as I did, but my father insisted. My father is very
old fashioned and is set in his ways, so my pregnancy was very wrong to him. You see, I had to
have you adopted. There was no way my father would
let me keep you.
    I must go now. Remember that I will love you
always and will always hold a place in my heart

for you. Please be happy and have a wonderful life.
                          All My Love,
                          Your Birthmother

Friends of birthparents are motivated to believe the third myth by their own feelings of compassion and a sense of inadequacy. Assisting a birthparent through the adoption experience requires tremendous knowledge and understanding of the dynamics of fear, guilt, and sorrow. Ill-prepared to handle the situation, especially the aftermath of the placement, friends often evade the subject. Not wanting to awaken their friend's anguish, they avoid the topic through rationalizing, "Carol and Jay have forgotten so don't remind them by talking about it."

Finally, adoptive parents seek the comfort of the third myth. Most adoptive parents (or their family members and friends) know stories of birthmothers who changed their minds and sought to regain custody. Therefore, many adoptive parents instinctively react to calm their fear of this scenario by denying the possibility that their child's birthparents could have a continued emotional bond to the child. They believe birthparents go away and forget because they want to believe that. As one adoptive father confirmed, "When I acknowledge that Jamie's birthmother still cares for him then I open up all the old scares that she might want him back."

Although we fully appreciate the powerful needs of others to maintain the myth that birthparents forget, we reject such an unfair and disproportionate burden being placed upon the birthparents. Perpetuating this myth prolongs the stereotype of uncaring and unfeeling baby makers (remember the first myth). Most importantly, the third myth denies birthparents post-adoption counseling from the adoption professional and emotional support from family and friends. This, in effect, abandons two people at a time when assistance is most needed during their natural mourning period. Without social support, birthparents are handicapped in their ability to resolve their decision and to constructively rebuild their lives.

We firmly reject the temptation by many adoption

intermediaries to provide little or no post-adoption counseling because of their belief in this myth. We have structured counseling and support groups to assist our birthparents. We also strive to help family members and friends of our birthparents by involving them in the therapy routinely provided after the child's adoption. Our objective is to help these individuals clarify and directly face the emotions that cause them to seek the solace of the third myth. When they no longer need to deny that birthparents spend a lifetime remembering their child, family members and friends can help the birthparents and themselves deal with a myriad of feelings.

A sister of one of our birthmothers wrote the following letter to the adoptive parents of her niece. She no longer has a need to rationalize away the depth of feelings awakened for herself and for her sister by the placement of "their" child. Neither woman will ever forget:

Dear Special Parents,

I'm really not sure how to start this letter. I am the birthmother's sister. I'm a year older than her, graduated from high school this year and plan to go to college in the future.

When I read the letter you wrote my sister, I felt so much joy that words couldn't express my feelings. We were all so happy to hear about the baby that, at that moment, the letter meant more to all of us than anything in the world. I know it was very hard for my sister to give her baby up, but I feel she did the best for the baby.

You both seem like such wonderful parents that it's like you were a gift from God.

I'm so overwhelmed that the baby was so lucky as to have such parents that I know will give her all the love that is humanly possible.

There were many nights that I cried myself to sleep hoping and praying that the baby would become a very special part of her adoptive parents' heart as she has for us.

I hope that you will continue to write my sister on how the baby is progressing.

If I'm not asking too much, could you give the baby a kiss and a hug for me? It would mean so much to me.

Thank you both for being such perfect parents. May God be with you all and protect you always.

                    Sincerely,
                    A thankful birthmother's sister

Besides working with the family members and friends of birthparents to counter the third myth, we counsel our adoptive parents to acknowledge and deal with their feelings toward birthparents. Frequently, adoptive parents harbor the notion that birthparents have a natural right to withdraw their consent to an adoption. It is commonly believed that birthparents can and often do successfully reclaim their children. Let us compare this belief to the legal realities.

Adoption in the United States is purely statutory in nature. Each state establishes its own regulations in this matter. As a general rule there must be strict compliance with the applicable state law in order to place a minor child into an adoptive family. Birthparents must voluntarily consent to the adoptive placement of their child and this is usually accomplished by executing with full understanding a formal surrender document.

Generally, birthparents have *no absolute right* to revoke their consent if their surrender was freely and voluntarily given. Moreover, under various adoption statutes, approval of the court is essential to withdrawal of a birthparent's consent. These laws give the court discretionary power to allow or refuse the request for withdrawal. The court exercises this discretion in the best interest of the child and in accordance with the reasonableness of each birthparent's claim.

A birthparent who does seek to withdraw a previously granted consent to adoption must show that good cause exists to set aside such consent. An attempted withdrawal based on whim or caprice or motivated solely by a change of heart or mind will not result in the consent being revoked. The birthparent has the burden to prove that the consent was procured by such circumstances as fraud, duress, undue influence, or overreaching. In actuality this burden is not frequently met, but if a birthparent does prove that consent was not freely executed, the court will allow the consent to be revoked. The very few such cases seem to receive disproportionate television and newspaper coverage, adding to the social perception that birthparents often withdraw their consent to an adoption. In total, although the fear of possibly losing the adoptee is very real to many adoptive parents, the legal reality is that revocation of properly executed surrenders happens much more frequently on soap operas than in real life.

Directly facing and discussing the fear of legally or emotionally losing the adoptee is a powerful start for the adoptive parent toward gaining insight. We appreciate the fact that only adoptive parents deal with the sometimes crippling thought that if the birthparents do change their minds, they as adoptive parents might lose a court battle. Uniqueness, however, does not make the adoptive parents' fears unmanageable or even unparalleled to other life experiences.

All parents routinely deal with fears surrounding the safety of their children. For example, parents do not hesitate to admit they worry that their child will be injured in a car wreck, and that motivates them to use seat belts. The same parents neither dwell on that apprehension nor deny its existence. Instead they simply accept it. We strive for our adoptive parents to have a similar acceptance of their fear of their child being reclaimed. We firmly believe that adoptive parents should not deny or dwell on anxieties that might tempt them to believe birthparents go away and forget, nor should adoptive parents expect their fears to totally disappear.

Recently, one of our adoptive couples felt secure enough to have a face-to-face meeting with the birthmother of their second son. Yet, they admitted to the fleeting thought, "We momentarily visualized her coming into the room with a gun to kidnap Chris." This couple can speak rationally of their momentary fantasy, but the fact is that they were still insecure even as they prepared to meet the young birthmother. Their fear may never totally disappear, and that is okay. The real positive for this couple is their ability to tell us and others about their experience without letting a soap-opera type fear dictate their decisions about their lives.

Once again, our experiences with the letter exchanges have been positive in relation to the third myth of adoption. Adoptive parents working with us learn firsthand that birth-parents do not forget. Letters also teach adoptive parents to accept their fears of reclaiming without seeking the solace of the third myth.

Lisa, an eighteen-year-old birthmother, wrote the following letter describing her continued love for her birthdaughter one year after placement:

> Dear adoptive family,
>
> I can't tell you how much your letter and picture at Christmas meant to me. I guess the hardest thing for me to deal with was giving my little girl to strangers. It really made me feel good to hear from you. I know sharing your feelings with me wasn't easy, but I feel so much more comfortable knowing a little bit about you.
>
> As her first birthday approaches I think about you often. I pray for you and hope that all is well. I don't want you to feel pressured, but if you feel comfortable writing, I am open to hear from you again.
>
> The birthfather and I are still together. He shares in wishing you all the best. He is working as a carpenter, and really likes his work. I am working as a night auditor, and am trying to get some college credit as well. I keep pretty busy.
>
> Please give your daughter an extra birthday hug and kiss from her birthmother and birthfather.
>
> With best wishes and all our love,
>
> Birthmother & Birthfather

The recipients of this letter might have been frightened by Lisa's obvious love for her birthchild and request for future information. Certainly, the time had passed for the myth to have worked its magic and made Lisa forget her little girl.

The adoptive parents, however, were not frightened. They took great comfort in learning about Lisa and about the birthfather of their daughter. Of course, these adoptive parents did not miss Lisa's reference to "your daughter," but that particular assurance is not as necessary as it once might have been. Their fears are no longer unmanageable.

Our letter exchanges have also clearly communicated that although birthparents may be sad or depressed at times, these feelings do not mean they would change their decision. Most birthparents feel like Debbie, who wrote three years after placement:

> I placed Craig for adoption so there would be as few disruptions in his life as possible. So my coming back to take him from his family would defeat my whole purpose.

Another birthparent, Valerie, expresses similar reassurance in her letter to the adoptive parents of her daughter. Valerie affirms them as parents, while still being interested in her child's development:

> Dear Sharon and Steve,
>   Yes, it has been a while since we have had contact, but now is a good time to say "hello" again. I am sure everything is going beautifully with the family and with our prayers it will stay that way always.
>   As time goes by, I keep thinking about that little angel ya'll have and how happy she must be. Surely she is growing prettier every minute. But she isn't a baby anymore, she's a little girl. She walks and talks and knows everyone's name. Soon she'll learn colors, numbers, and letters with the help of her smart parents and swell surroundings. But all I can remember is her as a tiny baby like the day she was born. I can't _even_ imagine her standing up (that's how long it's been)!!! I would like to fill my imaginations of a little girl instead of a baby very badly, but I think I need some help.

Can you please send me a short letter and tell
me how that little angel is doing? I would be so
happy it would make me cry with joy! It would be
an early Christmas present for me and my parents.
We would be ever so grateful. If it's not asking too
much may we also get a picture of her! It would
be nice to picture her as a little girl in my mind
when I pray for her.
Thank you.

Always,
Valerie

The adoptive parents who received this letter will no
longer perpetuate the myth that birthparents forget their
birthchild. They know Valerie will never forget her daughter,
but that fact is no longer alarming.

Other birthmothers share through their letters how they
respect both the adoptive parents of their child and the
integrity of that parent-child relationship. Kim, for example,
addressed her letter to "My Baby's Parents:"

To My Baby's Parents,
It's so hard for me to begin this letter, so much
I would like you to understand that giving my son
up for adoption was the hardest decision I ever had
to make. I am just so glad I was able to do it. No
mother likes to think her child would be better off
without her. But, I realize that isn't true. I couldn't
give my son everything I wanted him to have. And
I wanted him to have the world. But you could. You
were able to give him everything I wanted for him.
But what makes it even nicer was knowing that
you were doing everything because you love him
too! Not because you had to, but because you wanted
to. I know that bringing children up today is
challenging and involved. I realize you have your
work cut out for you. But I know everything will
work out fine. I believe in your new family.
I don't regret any decision I have made concerning my baby. It was hard letting him go. I know

it was in his best interest. I did it because I love
him and cared only about his interest, his life. I
will never forget my son, I never want to forget.
He will always remain a part of me. My love always
with him.

I realize he's your son now. We all have played
such a vital part in his beginning. I gave him life
and then I gave him to you. You will shape that
life and make him into a fine young man. I am
so glad he has you. I am so glad you're there for
him. I couldn't have found two better people to be
his parents if I had done the choosing myself.

After he was born, I started believing that God
does work in mysterious ways. He gave me the son
I had always dreamed of. Then He made it possible
for me to give my baby a family. Something I wanted
so much for him to have. And He gave you the child
you wanted so much.

I'd like to think God planned this from the
very beginning. I believe on September 23 I not only
gave birth to a beautiful baby boy, I gave birth to
a start of a family.

I will never be able to thank you enough for
everything, for just being there when I need you,
when my son needed you. I know that he's happy
and loved now with you both. I could not have asked
for anything more. I hope and pray your home and
lives are filled with nothing but love and laughter.
Thank you so much. I feel nothing but love and
good wishes for you both and your family.

> Gratefully and Sincerely
> Yours,
> Kim

Kim speaks of her love for the parents of her birthson
and the love was warmly received by Ron and Kathy. As
adoptive parents, Ron and Kathy might at times need to deal
with a recurrence of the thought that Kim will change her
mind. Both, however, have learned to calmly accept this as
part of parenthood.

The open communication and trust that can develop through the letter exchanges constitute a productive rejection of the third myth. The human tendency to believe and maintain a "forgetting" fiction is replaced by a healthy desire to know and to assist both birthparents. Most importantly, as adoptees hear about their birthparents, they will have the opportunity to learn accurate stories of continued love.

4

A Search for Roots, Not Different Parents

Myth Number Four:
"If the adoptee really loved his adoptive family, he would not have to search for his birthparents."

Curiosity and interest in one's past or future lineage speaks well of a healthy, inquisitive mind. The enthusiasm which greeted Alex Haley's *Roots* indicates that modern American society wholeheartedly endorses inquiring into one's heritage—unless you are an adoptee. For adoptees, yearning to know about their heritage is still disapprovingly labeled an ungrateful act.

The basis of the fourth myth of adoption—that curbs the adoptee's hunger to know his heritage—stems from a misguided desire to reward adoptive parents for their unselfish act of adopting. The myth's professed objective is to spare the two individuals who willingly labored to parent "someone else's child"—spare them the hurt of rejection from the child seeking his "real parents." The myth actually sets up scenarios of the present family unit being dismantled in favor of a new family. The most common picture is the ungrateful adoptee who abandons his adoptive parents to love his "natural mother."

The fourth myth is also designed to punish birthparents for an unwed parenthood. This time the myth's objective is to discipline the individuals who conceived a child but dared not to parent him. Society mandates a righteous punitive measure for such a "sin"—lifetime separation.

Tragically, the adoptee's welfare is ignored in both the rewarding and punishing aspects of the fourth myth. Adoptees are the only individuals in the United States denied knowledge of their genealogy. By the laws of most states, they are not allowed access to their original birth certificates, nor to the court records and adoption agency files of their adoption. These documents alone contain the identity of their birthparents and the social and medical histories that many adoptees seek to orient themselves in their own existence.

Through our post-adoption work, we daily encounter adoptees seeking accurate information about their origins and their genetic potential. Contrary to what advocates of the myth would have us believe, these are not unhappy adoptees running away from home and their nonunderstanding parents. These are adoptees who talk easily about contented childhoods and close family relationships. Yet they recount numerous unanswered questions about their biological identity. They report recurrent dreams about their "abandonment." They even have distorted fantasies and daydreams about their birthparents.

They have two universal questions: The simple one which non-adoptees would take for granted, "Who do I look like?" and then the loaded question that seeks confirmation of self-worth, "Why was I given away?" We have learned from these adoptees that the identity crisis of adolescence impacts the adoptee in unique ways. One adoptee recalled those turbulent years:

> I needed to know who I was, and what I was all about. But I had no way to find out.

Another adoptee, now twenty years old, related how she "set out" as a teenager to get pregnant and keep her baby. "I wanted a child because I desperately needed a bloodline. I needed to actually touch someone related to me."

Marriage and pregnancy can also frighten the adoptee. Some adoptees fear a possible incestuous marriage to a blood relative. Other adoptees, denied information about their genetic make up, worry about what kind of child they will conceive. "Will I pass on a crippling disease?" they wonder.

The search for a medical history is itself a need to be complete. Kelly, age thirty-two, recalls always being traumatized when going to a new doctor. Every new doctor would ask about her medical history and when she revealed that she was adopted, he would simply tear the medical history form in two. Each time, she was humiliated by such an overt reminder of the void in her background.

We have also observed how subsequent parenthood for the adoptee is usually a time of extreme joy. They finally know a "blood relative!" Adult adoptees, in fact, express an almost childlike delight in at last knowing someone who looks like them.

In sum, adoptees are not running away from their adoptive parents. Nor do they want to intrude in the birthparents' lives. They simply seek background information to untangle their pasts and help predict their future.

We reject the practice of the adoptee being blocked from his roots by restrictive laws and the social attitudes propagating the fourth myth. Betty Jean Lifton, a writer, experienced the terrible aloneness of being an adopted adult denied access to her genetic background. We share Ms. Lifton's belief that adoptees need a sense of continuity and belonging that may only come through their search for origins. Ms. Lifton wrote, in 1979:

> The struggle for a sense of identity is common to all of us. For an adoptee it takes on an uncommon dimension. Cut off from blood roots, the adoptee is often deeply troubled by feelings of abandonment and alienation. There is a sense of nonexistence, of never having been born.*

Unfortunately, today's adult adoptee has grown up in a society which still believes in the fourth myth. He has been conditioned to believe that he would be "ungrateful" to his

---

*Lifton, Betty Jean, *Lost & Found: The Adoption Experience,* New York, NY. The Dial Press, 1979.

adoptive parents if he searched. Thirsty for simple pieces of information but guilty about possibly hurting Mom and Dad, the adoptee is caught in an emotional tug-of-war. He must possess great strength and determination to actually pursue his search, and even then the actual process of searching is often frustrating and painful.

Regrettably, the adoption agency (which is generally one of the first places the adoptee goes for information) also subscribes to the fourth myth. The agency can be negative and punitive to the adoptee, saying, "Why do you want to search; aren't you happy with your adoptive parents?" or "You should be grateful—just think how much this will hurt your adoptive parents."

The adoptee is further blocked in his search by his own fears. Since he too has grown up with the messages of myth number one ("Your birthmother obviously doesn't care about you or she wouldn't have given you away") and number three ("Both your birthmother and birthfather have forgotten you"), the adoptee fears rejection by his birthparents. He most dreads an uncaring birthmother rejecting him a second time!

Again the adoption agency and professional intermediary support the myths by warning the adoptee that his birthmother wants confidentiality:

> What about your birthmother's rights—what if she doesn't want to be found?

The intermediary might even imply, with a kind of calculating cliché, that the adoptee will find something negative if he pursues his search.

One's roots and origins, no matter how apparently sordid in the eyes of middle-class laymen and professionals, are a part of a person's reality. Circumstances under which a birthparent relinquished a birthchild are invariably understandable if the facts and full truth of their life situation are known. Rarely, if ever, do birthparents give up that role without great reluctance and cost to themselves. Most often the welfare of their child is their main concern. To deny the adoptee access to these facts is to lock him into negative fantasizing about his birthparents and ultimately about himself.

Fear of the unknown can cripple any one of us in our search for personal growth; therefore, we hope adoption intermediaries and society in general will be able to free themselves from the fourth myth. The stress and negativism imposed by the mandate not to search should be lifted from the adult adoptee. He may have simple curiosity or a specific need to know his origins and genetic potential. We think that he, like any other adult, deserves that freedom of choice.

We also reject the fourth myth's attempt to protect "unselfish" adoptive parents. We admit that on first reflection, there is something threatening to a parent about a child wanting to go off and find his or her "real parents." It feels like a rejection, as if the adoptive parents were not all they should have been; but when examined from the perspective of the adoptee's need, good parenting involves encouraging the adoptee's curiosity and preparing him for all of life's independent searches.

Our experiences with adoptees convince us that the search for origins does not result in the adoptive parents losing their son or daughter. Adoptive parents and society must understand the role the adoptee's collective parents maintain—his birthparents gave him the reality of birth and heritage, and his adoptive parents give him the reality of parenting and nurturing. One cannot take the other's place. Each parent is real in a unique way; no parent is better or worse. The adoptee has a connection to all his parents which is as real as his life, given or nurtured.

Kelly, the adoptee we referred to earlier who was haunted by her lack of a medical history, did hunt for her answers. What she found was, first, a birthmother who could answer her questions about her medical background, and second, a sensitive person who—wondrously—looks like her. (She had always wondered where she got her "ethnic" nose.) In addition, Kelly found a friend to share numerous identical interests. Today, Kelly maintains ongoing contact with her birthmother. She described their relationship as two good friends, and like good friends they correspond and visit with each other regularly.

Kelly is quick to add she still considers her adoptive parents as her parents. That relationship is solidly built on a foundation of shared memories, mutual respect, and tender love. Her adoptive parents' nurturing and continued presence are as essential to Kelly today as was their support when she first braved a pursuit for answers. The fact that Kelly has ongoing contact with her birthmother does not signify that her adoptive parents have lost. Kelly's bond to her adoptive parents is not so fragile that the ties could be erased or weakened simply because Kelly likes or even learns to love the woman who gave her life.

Unfortunately, many adoptees who search for their origins do not share their pursuit with their adoptive parents. They fear that their parents will be hurt, so out of loyalty and love they do not talk of their need to know. It is especially sad to hear Dick, a twenty-seven-year-old adoptee, tell a room full of adoptive parents how his exploration for and actual meeting with his birthmother reaffirmed his admiration and tenderness for his adoptive parents. Yet his adoptive parents cannot share this knowledge. Dick has never been able to tell them he was "ungrateful" enough to search for and find his birthmother, so he cannot now share his stronger love for them.

Some adoptees locked in by loyalty and the myth choose to wait to conduct their search until after their adoptive parents die. This ability to set aside one's own needs in order to protect a loved one from possible pain reflects their deep love and loyalty. Amy, for example, is a twenty-year-old adoptee who has a great desire to look for her birthparents but she also refuses to hurt her adoptive parents. She thinks her search would hurt them because they have never been able to talk about her birthmother without tears in their eyes. Amy has chosen to postpone any inquiry until after her parents' deaths. Since her adoptive parents are older than her birthparents, Amy is willing to risk that her birthparents will still be alive at that time.

Unfortunately, the fourth myth has prevented Dick and Amy from openly and honestly talking to their adoptive parents. Dick's and Amy's parents will be forever denied the opportunity to fully appreciate the depth of their children's love. Additionally, these parents are robbed of an opportunity to grow. They will never learn that just as parents can love more than one child, so too can an adoptee, like Dick or Amy, love more than one mother or one father.

The issue is not which set of parents has the greater right, nor which set the adoptee will love the most. A loved child will mature into a loving adult who will not waste that love, but who may share that love in many different ways. Adoptees frequently tell us that seeking and finding their birthparents does not lessen their love for their adoptive parents (who remain Mom and Dad). Permission to know one's heritage only makes the adoptee love his adoptive parents more—for giving him freedom and for trusting his love.

We also firmly refuse to accept the punishment aspect of the fourth myth, reserved for "sinful" birthmothers. Adoption laws often block birthparents, even more than adult adoptees, from searching and finding. If a birthparent ventures to search, too often curiosity is hatefully labeled "unnatural" by busy intermediaries and conservative judges. Remember, the third typical myth would have a birthparent believe, "You should have forgotten by now."

We support the birthparents' desire and prerogative to someday know their child. We find their curiosity to be a healthy reflection of their caring for their birthchild. In addition, such curiosity is reassuring for the adoptee afraid to be twice rejected, afraid to start his own search.

Russell, a nineteen-year-old birthfather, relates his need to someday meet his daughter in a personal letter to her. His love clearly deserves no punishment:

Dear Daughter,

I want to start this letter by telling you how sorry I am, although I am not sorry for placing you for adoption, I am only sorry that we cannot spend our lives together. Although I only really knew you for a day, I will miss you, and I will always have you in my heart.

The situation between your birthmother and me was that we both loved you very much, but we didn't love each other. We could give you love but not a home. A child needs a home with two people who care and love that child together. This your birthmother and I could not provide, and it is this that I am sorry for. Our decision was a difficult one, because it is not easy to give up one so dear. The only way we could do this was because we knew through adoption you would get the chance you really deserve to grow up healthy and happy. I pray that you will forgive us and understand why we placed you for adoption.

By the time you read this letter you will have grown enough to hopefully know why we did what we did. Your birthmother and I love you very much. I hope this letter will help you as much as it has helped me. I shall never forget you, and I will always have the hope that someday we will meet, so that we can both satisfy our curiosity, and see what each other is really like. Daughter, have a wonderful life, and I Love You.

Love Always,
Your Birthfather
Russell

We reject a myth that would punish Russell or any birth-parent who feels, "We could give you love but not a home." Concerned United Birthparents (CUB) probably sums the birthparent's right and need for information most dramatically in the following statement:

> **To never know your birthchild is to spend a lifetime in anguish of forever wondering, a punishment disproportionate to the crime of giving birth and allowing another to parent the child.***

We work to counter the fourth myth by first exploring with our adoptive parents the dynamics of the adoptee's need to search. An adoptee's curiosity and fundamental

---

*Campbell, Lee H (Editor), *Understanding the Birthparent,* Milford, MA. Concerned United Birthparents, Inc., 1978.

quest for roots is shared by everyone. For the adoptee, however, two "other" parents exist somewhere. This fact alone converts the quest for roots from an intellectual pursuit to a dramatic life experience. Their search is to find a sense of continuity, to avoid the grief of permanent separation and loss, and to learn a biological identity.

Once we explore the adoptee's need to search for his or her answers, we assist our adoptive parents to examine the unsettling fears triggered by this reality. Do they still believe their child would not search if he loved them enough? As with all fears, we encourage our adoptive parents to acknowledge and experience them, not deny them.

Fears that they will lose their child to his "real parents" or even that their child will find out "bad things" about his birthparents are unique to adoptive parents. But these fears can be managed. Understanding the adoptee's need to search does help the adoptive parent. Most frequently we see our parents transforming the hurt of the fourth myth to the awareness and sensitivity displayed in the following letter:

Dear Birthmother of my Daughter,

I've been wanting to write you but I am sure you realize finding the words to express my feelings is difficult. Sunday in church the thoughts of you ran through my mind as I was again reminded of God's love that he gave his only Son for me. I compared your gift of love to His. It's a gift of love that is a continuing gift of love, love that grows daily. It's a gift of love that I'm sure was a great price for the giver and for that we are more grateful than we can possibly express.

Getting this baby was a long and painful process for us. I'll spare you the details but I want you to know how deeply wanted this child is and therefore, how special. The joy when we first saw her was a high that I've never experienced. It was love at first sight for both of us. . . .

I have some hopes for your future, too. I hope your future brings the realization of your goals. Your continuing welfare will always be in my prayers. I'm sure you would like to close off this episode of your life although I don't mean forgetting. I'm sure you never will but I want to leave you with the confidence that our daughter is in a home where she is truly wanted and where she will grow up surrounded by love. I also want you to know that when she learns about you, I will do my best to convey to her that it was your love for her that has given us the chance to grow as a loving family and that she can love you and be grateful to you also.

Now for something painful I feel is necessary to tell you. Someday our daughter may want to find you. I will do my best to bring her up confident of her being loved and respecting your right to your life which does not need to reopen old wounds. I want her to respect that right of yours, however, if when she is grown she feels it is necessary to find you I will not try to prevent her doing so and will even help. I'm sure you must have considered this possibility and I felt compelled to tell you how I feel about it. Should you choose to respond to my letter you may want to say something about your feelings on this matter that I would be able to share with our daughter to help her understand.

I'm having difficulty in finding words to close this letter. I want you to know something of the fantastic enjoyment and pleasure I am experiencing in the daily care of my happy, healthy, growing daughter and her father's deep pride and loving care. We wish you joy, love and peace in your life and from the bottom of our hearts we thank you for the joy, love and peace you have given us.

> Your daughter's
> Mother and Father

As the preceding letter indicates, adoptive parents working with us no longer regard an adoptee's need to search as a negative statement about their ability to parent. Nor do they believe the myth's prediction of an inevitable loss. One assertive mother soundly rejected the fourth myth and the people who believe it when she commented,

It only hurts if adoptive parents can't separate themselves from their child's need for a biological identity.

As this adoptive mother understands, effective adoptive parenting involves the realization that adoptees search for their origins, not for replacement parents.

Once adoptive parents deal with their own fears, they, too, seek out the birthparents who can supply the missing answers. Adoptive parents want accurate data about their child's biological family history. Our experience shows that adoptees who grow up having "I don't know" as answers to their questions begin to distrust the adoptive parents. "What are they hiding from me and why?" they frequently question. Therefore, no secrecy can be allowed here because our adoptive parents want information the adoptee can trust.

Through our letter exchanges adoptive parents are rarely forced to say, "I don't know." They have a ready and open communication channel to the persons best able to answer. The family structure is not inadvertently weakened by unanswerable questions. The adoptee, in fact, is supported in his pursuit for origins and a whole identity by his collective parents.

Actually, openness and ongoing communication between all members of the adoption drama nullify the need for a myth designed to protect and punish. Adoptive parents need no protection from a loss or hurt that will never occur. Caring birthparents deserve no punishment for their act of creating life.

Janet and Ray are adoptive parents who want to develop a trusting and strong family bond with their new daughter, Ann. They no longer harbor the fourth myth so they both feel that it is natural for intimate members of the adoption drama to want to reach out and know each other. They wrote Ann's birthmother the following letter the night before they brought Ann home:

It is the night before we see our new adopted
daughter for the first time. There is absolutely no
way on earth that we can express to you all the
joy that we feel. Tomorrow, without a doubt, is one
of the happiest days of our lives!

In all of our joy our thoughts are with you.
The adoption agency had given us more of an insight
as to how you must feel. We imagine the decision
you made to give her up was the most difficult one
you've made in your life. We wish there was a way
to alleviate your sorrow. We hope, however, you may
find some comfort in sharing our joy and in knowing that we so deeply love this little girl even though
we haven't seen her. We plan to tell her all about
you; how kind, gentle, and unselfish you must be
to forsake your own happiness for hers.

We thank you, kind lady, for the joy you have
brought to us and vow to treasure and love the precious gift you have bestowed upon us. May you find
only happiness and God Bless You!

Janet and Ray, as do our other adoptive parents, reject
the fourth myth's mandate of no searching. Ann will be raised
with all the knowledge her collective parents can provide. In
addition, Ann will not be told the "chosen child" story that
reflects society's biased fourth myth—"a child specially
chosen and given sufficient love by adoptive parents will not
want to know her heritage."

Our children were born to real persons, not magically
chosen from a crib in an agency, somewhere, one day. They
each have a birthmother and a birthfather who care and who
will not forget. They have heritages and genetic potentials
that they can claim. As nurturing parents and concerned
professionals, we must do everything we can to help our
adoptees to grow up healthy and whole. That includes helping them find any missing pieces of their own precious
identities.